HISTORIC INDIA

GREAT AGES OF MAN

A History of the World's Cultures

HISTORIC INDIA

by

LUCILLE SCHULBERG

and

The Editors of TIME-LIFE BOOKS

TIME-LIFE BOOKS, NEW YORK

THE AUTHOR: Lucille Schulberg is a staff writer for TIME-LIFE BOOKS. Her work has been published in such popular periodicals as *Harper's Bazaar* and *The Saturday Evening Post*. After World War II she wrote and announced her own radio program in Europe for the American Red Cross; she also authored a radio play about India that was presented on NBC. For years she has been a student of Indian culture and has traveled extensively through the subcontinent, as well as through the neighboring areas of Asia that have been important to Indian history.

THE CONSULTING EDITOR: Leonard Krieger, University Professor at the University of Chicago, was formerly Professor of History at Yale. Dr. Krieger is the author of *The German Idea of Freedom* and *The Politics of Discretion* and co-author of *History*, written in collaboration with John Higham and Felix Gilbert.

THE COVER: An elegant court lady, exquisitely painted by an 18th Century miniaturist of the Punjab hills, dangles a pearly bauble before an attentive pet peacock.

TIME-LIFE BOOKS

EDITOR
Maitland A. Edey

EXECUTIVE EDITOR
Jerry Korn

TEXT DIRECTOR   ART DIRECTOR
Martin Mann   Sheldon Cotler

CHIEF OF RESEARCH
Beatrice T. Dobie

PICTURE EDITOR
Robert G. Mason

Assistant Text Directors:
Harold C. Field, Ogden Tanner
Assistant Art Director: Arnold C. Holeywell
Assistant Chief of Research: Martha Turner

PUBLISHER
Rhett Austell

General Manager: Joseph C. Hazen Jr.
Planning Director: John P. Sousa III
Circulation Director: Joan D. Manley
Marketing Director: Carter Smith
Business Manager: John D. McSweeney
Publishing Board: Nicholas Benton,
Louis Bronzo, James Wendell Forbes

GREAT AGES OF MAN

SERIES EDITOR: Russell Bourne
Editorial Staff for *Historic India:*
Deputy Editor: Carlotta Kerwin
Text Editors: William Frankel,
Anne Horan
Picture Editor: John Paul Porter
Designer: William Rose
Assistant Designer: Raymond Ripper
Staff Writers: Marianna P. Kastner,
John von Hartz, Victor Waldrop,
Bryce Walker, Edmund White
Chief Researcher: Peggy Bushong
Researchers: Carol Isenberg,
Johanna Zacharias, Linda Wolfe,
Susan Grafman, Kathleen Brandes,
Val Chu, Elizabeth Evans,
Helen Greenway, Helen Lapham,
Diana Lea, Sigrid von Huene,
Arlene Zuckerman
Art Assistant: Anne Landry

EDITORIAL PRODUCTION
Color Director: Robert L. Young
Assistant: James J. Cox
Copy Staff: Marian Gordon Goldman,
Barbara Hults, Florence Keith
Picture Department: Dolores A. Littles,
Joan Lynch
Traffic: Arthur A. Goldberger

The following individuals and departments of Time Inc. gave valuable aid in the preparation of this book: the Chief of the LIFE Picture Library, Doris O'Neil; the Chief of the Time Inc. Bureau of Editorial Reference, Peter Draz; the Chief of the TIME-LIFE News Service, Richard M. Clurman; Correspondents Margot Hapgood and Barbara Moir (London), James Shepherd, Stephanie Markham, Francine Zuzzolo and Minnie Chandihok (New Delhi), Ann Natanson (Rome), Maria Vincenza Aloisi and Joan Dupont (Paris), Elisabeth Kraemer (Bonn), Erik Amfitheatrof (Tokyo), Jean Bratton (Madrid) and Traudl Lessing (Vienna).

CONTENTS

INTRODUCTION

The genius of India, said Jawaharlal Nehru, consists of synthesis. This book, a broad survey of Indian history and culture from the Third Millennium B.C. to the 17th Century A.D., bears witness to the keenness of Nehru's generalization. The more one studies Indian history, the clearer it becomes that no single basic Indian culture has been developed and elaborated through the ages. Instead, successive cultural influences have fused together to form the fascinating country and intricate way of life we know as India and Hinduism. The wonder of India is that these layers of fused elements have produced not an amorphous collection of hostile groups, but a cohesive Hindu society with a unique social structure, art and world view.

This society is, in fact, one of the most closely knit in world history. For an Indian, all action is ritual, all art is symbolic of religious ideas, all worship is an expression of life, all life is a facet of the Eternal. Underlying these identities is the Indian's sense of a spirit that pervades all things and the Indian's worship of this all-pervading spirit. An Indian must worship; some spend their lives in worshipful meditation, others make do with homage to a stone or a tree. Through a combination of worship, ritual and religion, Indians have succeeded in synthesizing extraordinarily diverse forces and influences.

In words and pictures, this book shows how the synthesizing process flowered into a varied and creative civilization during five millennia. The civilization's creative power was first seen in religion, in which the development of three great creeds—Hinduism, Buddhism and Jainism—provides a record that no other culture has ever matched. This creativity was next seen in art, architecture and literature. And in the social order, Indian civilization created elaborate structures of caste and class-structures which can be explained, if not justified, by India's overall world view.

Like all human developments, these are linked to specific events in time, specific fusions and flowering of cultures. The earliest and perhaps the greatest of all Indian fusions took place between the prehistoric Harappan Culture—one of the oldest civilizations known to archeologists—and that of the Aryans, who invaded the subcontinent sometime after 1500 B.C. Later periods represent a great flowering of the Indian spirit. The first was that of the Mauryan Age of the Third Century B.C., dominated by a patron of Buddhism, the Emperor Ashoka. A second occurred during the Fourth and Fifth Centuries A.D., when art, literature and science reached their highest points under the reigns of the Gupta emperors. Finally, the book discusses the 16th and 17th Century Age of the Mughals and Emperor Akbar, who among later Muslim monarchs most nearly approached the Hindu ideal of an all-India ruler.

A warm word of praise should be added for the author of the book, the editors of TIME-LIFE BOOKS and consultant Ainslie T. Embree for the skill and grace with which they have interwoven the many strands of this rich cultural tapestry to form a lucid and fascinating design.

PERCIVAL SPEAR
Fellow of Selwyn College
University Lecturer in History
Cambridge University

MTS.

PLATEAU

HIMALAYAS

Patna

PLAIN

Konarak

BAY OF BENGAL

HISTORIC INDIA
Traditional regions
and major sites

1
AN ENDURING TRADITION

Historic India is not a country. It is a culture, one of the oldest and most consistent on earth. That culture has been a contemporary to almost all civilizations. It existed, in nascent form, when the sun rose on Egypt's first kingdom in the Fourth Millennium B.C. Well developed, it was present when the sun sparkled on classical Greece in the Fifth Century B.C. and set on the British Empire in this century. The culture consists predominantly of a religion and a mode of living called Hinduism.

Hinduism took root, grew and reached a confident maturity in the vast period this book describes—the time between the Third Millennium B.C. and the 17th Century A.D. Toward the end of this long period, it faced its first serious cultural challenge when Muslims, men of an equally mature way of life, ruled most of the land of India. Yet through all of historic India, the great power of Hindu culture has been manifest.

Across the world and through the centuries India has made her greatness known. The spirit of Hinduism first intrigued the West centuries before the beginning of the Christian era, and it has been a source of wonder and speculation for our philosophers and poets ever since. Ancient Greeks and Romans admired the richness and the royal perquisites of two of the great Indian empires (the Mauryan of the Third Century B.C. and the Gupta of the Fourth and Fifth Centuries A.D.). Buddhism, which originated in India in the Sixth Century B.C., went with missionaries to the ancient courts of China and Japan, where it reached its most elaborate of several varying forms. From the Second to the Ninth Century A.D., Hinduism was the major civilizing force throughout Southeast Asia.

Despite these triumphs, historic India has often puzzled or frustrated Western observers. Again and again, such observers have reported their sense of a vast cultural and psychological distance between India and the West. Here is an admonition from Alberuni, an 11th Century Muslim scholar who dedicated 13 years to studying India.

The reader must always bear in mind that the Hindus entirely differ from us in every respect. . . . They differ from us in every

A NATURE-GODDESS, *sculpted in the 11th or 12th Century A.D., embodies the spirit of a tree. Throughout the long history of civilization in India, sacred trees—as well as certain rivers, mountains, plants and animals—were worshiped as aspects of a universe that was considered inherently divine.*

thing which other nations have in common. . . . They totally differ from us in religion. . . . In all manners and usages they differ from us to such a degree as to frighten their children with us.

Many Westerners tend to criticize India's differences as shortcomings. Ignoring the integrity and historical validity of Indian culture, Westerners have criticized the Hindu attitude toward progress, which Hindus regard as impossible beyond predetermined limits; or the Indian insistence that individual men must follow hereditary occupations set down and perpetuated by the caste system; or India's inability, except on rare occasions, to rise above the political level of petty warring states.

Such attitudes and failures may indeed seem puzzling, even reprehensible, in light of the Western legacy from Judea and Greece. In fact, however, they stem from India's own legacy and do not represent waywardness or mystery so much as they represent profound differences between Indian and Western beliefs. Truly basic beliefs are rarely discussed among us; many of them lie so deep as to be subconscious or inarticulate. But certain basic beliefs or concepts reflect vast differences between India and the West.

For example, the Western concept of time is different from the Indian. Westerners view time as a steady, straight progression. We "know" that there is past, present and future, and we "know" that when a moment is gone, it is gone forever. An event occurring now is fully believed to be in some respect different from similar events of the past and events of the future. Hindus "know" exactly the opposite. For them, everything that happens has happened before and will happen again; anything that has not happened will never happen. Hindus view time as a revolving circle, without beginning and without end, and they hold that everything in the universe, including

A JAUNTY DANCING GIRL, *naked except for her necklace and bangles, was cast in bronze in the Indus Valley in the Second Millennium B.C. The figure's Negroid features are thought to be characteristic of some of the earliest inhabitants in the area.*

the gods or God, is bound together within the constantly repeated cycle of time.

Most Westerners adhere to a concept of absolute truth: a fact is either true or false, and what is true for one man is true for all. Hindus believe that there are many kinds of truth, truths that are different for every age, every occupation, every class of men. Indeed, one of Hinduism's objections to Judaism, Christianity and Islam is that they preach one truth for all men.

Like many Westerners, Hindus believe in the idea that every good act reaps a good result and every evil act an evil one—but Hinduism goes far beyond the West in its belief. The Hindu law of ethical cause and effect, called karma, is considered neither man-made nor god-made; for Hindus, it is a natural law, as impersonal, impartial and inexorable as the law of gravity.

Though many, perhaps most, Westerners believe in an afterlife, they also believe that a man leads only one life here on earth. Hindus, on the other hand, believe firmly in the idea of rebirth, or reincarnation. Transmigrating from one body to the next, a Hindu soul gathers the good or evil fruits of the acts of previous lifetimes.

Indians also are deeply committed to a concept called dharma, which has no direct counterpart in the West. Students of Hinduism have rendered the term as "moral code," and "sacred obligation," but the most accurate English equivalent is perhaps "duty," for dharma is the dutiful way of life. For a religious Westerner, a righteous life may be either its own reward or an assurance of a happy afterlife. For a Hindu, it is intricately bound up with other Hindu concepts. Like Hindu truths, dharmas are different for different people, and they influence karma and reincarnation. By following his dharma correctly in each life, a man affects his karma so that he may be reborn into better lives during the repeated cycles of time.

What is so unique about historic India is not one or another of these basic beliefs, but the entire fabric of Hinduism—of which these concepts are the vital strands. Taken together, the principles are guidelines for living, as well as tenets of a religious faith. And they are all the more difficult for Westerners to comprehend because they are inseparably intertwined with a distinctive social arrangement: the caste system. Together these conceptual and social strands constitute the very warp and woof of Hinduism.

Caste is the living enactment of the Hindu ideas of difference—different truths, different lives through rebirth, different karmas and dharmas. In the Hindu caste system, the unit of society has not been the individual, but the group he belonged to. All people were divided into hereditary groups that were socially isolated from the others by elaborate regulations and restrictions and by hierarchal position. Status was and is intrinsic to Hinduism; everything Hindu has a "higher" or "lower" standing, and every caste has a social standing superior or inferior to that of every other caste.

The structure of caste and the basic ideas of Hindu philosophy have contributed to almost every accomplishment—and failure—of historic India. In turn, that unique combination of social structure and philosophical ideas was the result of contributions from a bewildering variety of sources. Just as historic Europe developed its character through invasions of many peoples and diverse philosophies, so India owes its culture to onslaughts of new people whose ideas made them the unwitting progenitors of Hinduism.

Yet the molding of Indian civilization followed a pattern quite different from that of the West. In Europe during the Age of Barbarians (400 to 1050 A.D.), small groups either fought each other to a finish or merged into larger groups. The Celts of Britain, for example, were driven out of their homeland by invading Germanic peoples, who then established an Anglo-Saxon culture in Britain; the Anglo-Saxons were conquered by the Normans, and the result was England and an English people. It was impossible for European tribes remaining within the same territory to coexist; they invariably merged with one another. But in India—perhaps because an enormous number of dissimilar peoples *had* to find a way to live together—separate coexistence, not merger, became the clue to survival.

The land that has accepted such a great variety of unlike immigrants is huge—a peninsula so large that it is often called a subcontinent—but few lands have had to reconcile so many different racial strains, so many unlike social patterns and such a sheer multitude of people. By the end of the Fourth Century B.C. India's population had already reached 100 million. Many of these people were descendants of invaders; and in later centuries, other invaders came to India. Quickly or slowly, all the invaders and all their descendants became parts of the mosaic of historic India.

On first glance it may not be immediately apparent how new arrivals reached the interior of India. The Indian peninsula is nearly sealed off from the rest of the world by the towering Himalayas and the Hindu Kush mountain range, which together form the northern boundary of India—a boundary that is virtually a great wall as much as 150 miles thick, 2,000 miles long and 25,000 feet (or nearly five miles) high. But the mountains are not so impassible as their awesome girth suggests. Melting snows course down them to form rivers; the rivers have carved out a series of passes—some of which are as spectacular as the mountains themselves—and these passes have allowed invading tribes free entrance from the northwest since the start of India's history.

The migrants came down through the mountain passes, leaving behind them the endless peaks and chasmlike valleys of the towering Hindu Kush and the Himalayas. Emerging from some twisting gorge, such as the 34-mile-long Khyber Pass, they first encountered the hilly region of the Punjab. Traveling southeast, they found the land leveling out. For the first time in their lives, perhaps, they saw unbroken horizons in all directions. At this point, the migrants would be in the fertile Indo-Gangetic plain, which sweeps across the subcontinent in a great arc that, like the mountains that lie to the north, measures 2,000 miles from west to east and 150 to 200 miles from north to south.

And for the first time, such migrants discovered the Indian sun, a blazing fury. They could soon shed their shaggy clothes of animal skins and their warm leg-wrappings, following the lead of people already settled in this climate, and learn to wear the *dhoti*, a cotton cloth swathed around the waist. During the few months of the winter when the weather turned cool, they added a warm shawl about the head and shoulders.

Once in the Indo-Gangetic plain, some migrants went southwestward along the Indus River and found themselves in the region called the Sind—a cul-de-sac that is cut off from India's heartland by the huge Thar Desert. Luckier ones moved southeastward, on the lush path that lies between the rambling Ganges River and the foothills of the Himalayas. Continuing southeastward, they would arrive at the Bay of Bengal, where the Ganges delta was eventually to provide the great natural ocean harbor of Calcutta.

Traveling south from the plain by an alternate route, some migrants followed the Chambal River to enter a different kind of land. They would be on the Deccan plateau, a harsh, infertile grassland sloping west to east and broken by scrub and clumps of trees. East and west, at the borders of

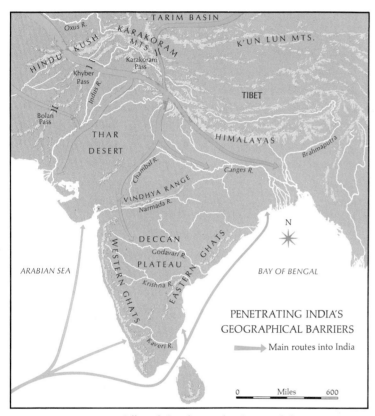

PENETRATING INDIA'S
GEOGRAPHICAL BARRIERS

→ Main routes into India

0   Miles   600

HISTORIC ROUTES, *some followed for thousands of years, led waves of new-comers into India. By land, most immigrants entered through the mountain passes in the northwest and then fanned out. By water, foreigners approached India across the Arabian Sea and ranged along both the east and west coasts.*

the Deccan, were more mountain ranges, the Ghats—so-called for the passes *(ghats)* that penetrate them—and narrow coastal plains. There the peninsula is shaped like an arrowhead, pointing south to the sea; its edges consist of tropical beaches stretching back into lush, green foliage.

The migrants who ventured south of the fertile Indo-Gangetic plain, whether just onto the high plateau or all the way to the coast, found themselves in a hostile world. This land was difficult to invade or control. Just getting into it was no easy task: a junglelike river valley of the Narmada, and a high escarpment, the Vindhya Mountains, cut the Deccan off from the Indo-Gangetic plain. Once the invaders reached the plateau, they faced new difficulties. The monsoon winds—cool and dry in the winter, drenching in the summer, always uncertain in the time of their coming—made either farming or herding a risky business. And only some straggling migrants continued southward through the Deccan, for innumerable rivers flowed from west to east across the land—rivers just wide enough to make the prospect of crossing look formidable.

Naturally enough, most of the people who entered India at the northwest mountain passes stopped north of the Deccan. For the few who penetrated the plateau and continued still farther, a completely new country unfolded. South of the Deccan the land slopes downward to the sea, forming a low, temperate coastal plain. This is today the land of the dark-skinned Dravidian people, whose ancestors were among the earliest migrants to India, and whose physical characteristics and social customs still prevail. Migrants from the north who later came to southern India never outnumbered or overwhelmed the Dravidian population. But they share with the Dravidians—and with all Hindus today—a reverence for the last possible spot that migrants could reach on the subcontinent: the southern tip of the great Indian landmass, now called Cape Comorin, where the white sand of the Arabian Sea, the black sand of the Bay of Bengal and the red sand of the Indian Ocean meet.

Whoever the first Dravidian people may have been, however and whenever they reached southern India, they must have encountered other peoples already settled on the land. For there is evidence that, before the dawn of history, the vast and segmented territories of the south supported Stone Age cave dwellers who are thought to have been Negroid and who left the first archeological traces. These early inhabitants of India had cultural characteristics at which we can only guess, but one characteristic we may assume: they were fiercely protective of their way of life and determined to preserve it against the competing life-patterns of those who entered their territory. Somehow, against all the odds, pockets of primitive peoples still exist in India, clinging to their age-old ways. Some of these groups have matrilinear societies ruled entirely by women—a structure their forebears no doubt observed as well. But they live side by side with patrilinear societies, where a man is head of the family and a male chief heads the social unit. This and other features of society were brought by later migrants.

By 1500 B.C. a long series of invasions had got under way. A main source of new peoples was Central Asia, which, as one historian puts it, was periodically "in ferment, bubbling with activity like some human volcano . . . throwing off streams of human lava." But for India, always so strangely vulnerable to invasion, migrating peoples could come from anywhere and everywhere. From the north and from the west, Indo-Europeans, Persians, Greeks, Scythians, Huns, Arabs, Turks, Mongols and uncountable others flowed in. For thousands and thousands of years, migrants or

marauders moved in through the northwest passes, wandered to the fertile plains and were trapped, so to speak. Once on the peninsula, they might settle or they might be restless, but they would not leave. Their descendants stayed in India forever.

If most of these peoples had been even somewhat related—or if the influx had ever stopped—India today might be a region where one religion or one life-style predominated. Similar peoples would have homogenized into a unified population and one mainspring idea could have governed them all. But always pouring in were completely different kinds of people at completely different levels of culture. There were black and white and yellow races. There were nomads, traders and armies. There were large, refined societies with poets and troubadours, and there were tiny clans of still primitive root-grubbers. Through Hinduism, India found room for them all.

Hinduism did not absorb these people; it enfolded them. Any group with special customs could be dropped into India and, by living apart, live amicably side by side with those already there. The new group then became a caste of its own. Occasionally social reformers who strove to weaken or destroy the caste system arose—only to discover that their splinter groups fell into the caste pattern: as anticaste groups, they formed new castes in the old society.

India's characteristic refusal to act as a sort of social blending-machine has always seemed peculiar to most non-Indians; to many, her separation of groups and isolation of people by caste has seemed peculiarly inhuman. But the caste system may have produced the only reasonable way for India to make an orderly process of growth. While inherently different groups could live their intimate lives distinctively and separately from the others, they could all at the same time contribute their work to the commonweal.

A PASSAGE TO INDIA *for migrants and conquerors was afforded by mountain passes between the 16,000-foot peaks of the Hindu Kush, near the border of modern Afghanistan. This 80-mile-long gorge, still used by wandering goatherds, was part of the route taken by Alexander the Great in 329 B.C.*

From the rich and wildly heterogeneous mixture of peoples that is India burst repeated explosions of culture. Hindu art, literature and science made truly golden ages of the Mauryan Empire in the Third Century B.C. and the Gupta Empire in the Fourth and Fifth Centuries A.D. Some 1,200 years later, Muslim tradition—which was influenced but never overwhelmed by Hinduism—created yet another period of glory in the Mughal Empire.

In the Mauryan period the vitality of Indian life is reflected in achievements in stone sculpture, an art as old as the foundations of Hinduism itself. Centuries later, during the Gupta period, the great religious sculpture of India, both Buddhist and Hindu, gave witness to Hinduism at its height. Gupta poetry and drama, written in India's classic Sanskrit language, are considered peers of the finest Western literature, and it was Gupta science that gave the world the concept of zero, and the so-called Arabic numerals.

In the time of the Mughal Empire, India displayed an ability to combine its Hindu culture, which was by then ancient, with that of the Muslims, who for eight centuries had been moving into the subcontinent. The Mughal Age glittered with exquisite Indo-Islamic painting, pulsated with Indo-Islamic music and, perhaps most memorably, endowed future generations with masterpieces of Indo-Islamic architecture, the most celebrated of which is the Taj Mahal, with its glorious dome, marble façades and jeweled inlays.

Cultural splendor is not the only product of India's diversity and separateness: political disunity has also been a constant and plaguing result. Hundreds of tiny states—kingdoms, principalities, the holdings of petty nobles—have proliferated to a degree that makes the fragmented Europe of medieval times seem positively monolithic.

This diversity has made India one of the most resilient of lands. Though there have been enough dynastic wars, palace revolts and popular uprisings in historic India to fill a library of history books, no recorded wars ever turned the whole land against itself. India's flexible character has always contrasted with the brittleness characteristic of Europe: at different times powerful kingdoms have dominated Europe and presented a certain brilliant face to the world; such kingdoms have shattered under the impact of new political ideas and popular tensions. But India is not brittle politically; history has effected few disruptions in its political pattern of numerous small states—a pattern that has prevailed for over 3,000 years.

Historic India is not brittle philosophically either. Indeed, Hinduism's strength is its resiliency. It bends to fulfill the varying needs of the land's dissimilar peoples. For millennia traders and travelers—and invaders—have provided almost continuous contact between India and the world outside, and as a result India's intellectuals have been exposed to the philosophies of other cultures in many eras. Yet, through the ages, Indians who could brilliantly analyze other attitudes adhered to their own point of view.

Hinduism seems to have given the people of India extraordinarily satisfactory answers to questions that have concerned men since they began to think: What is man, what is nature, what is God? Why does man live? How should he best live with himself, with other men, with the mysteries of nature and the cosmos?

These are hardly questions that occupy the daily thought of people in any country, but they are questions whose answers help to form the culture of the country and affect the least sophisticated person in it. India's indigenous answers to questions about the universe and humanity have permitted millions of people to come to terms with existence and to understand each other in a manner that is one of the world's greatest wonders.

THE FABLED VALE OF KASHMIR, *with its "floating gardens," lies beneath the mists of the Karakoram.*

THE MANY LANDS OF INDIA

Physically, the huge subcontinent of India is not one land at all. From north to south it is a sprawling mosaic of cloud-piercing mountains and rolling plains, blistering desert and placid lakes, tapering off between fertile shorelines beset by treacherous tides. In many sectors a cruel sun and monsoon rains take turns holding the land in sway—the sun drawing up every drop of moisture, the monsoon causing devastating floods. The inhabitants of India's varied regions are equally varied—men and women of all colors and creeds, many of them descendants of Central Asian, Near Eastern and European peoples who came to, and were finally absorbed by, the all-encompassing land. The vast majority are followers of Hinduism, which, like India itself, has proved diverse and resilient enough to embrace its followers in a common bond.

A VALLEY IN KASHMIR

HIGHLANDS:
ENTRY AND SOURCE

In northern India the mountains dominate the land. For 1,400 miles along the northern frontier rise the massive Himalayas, a frigid, craggy barrier up to 150 miles wide—studded with the tallest mountains in the world; in the northwest the ranges of the Karakoram and the Hindu Kush are only slightly less awesome.

To the Hindus the mountains symbolize the immortality of divine power and the source of all India's life. Its major rivers, the Indus and the Ganges, spring from the mountains' snowy mantles. On its way, the clear water that runs down from the peaks irrigates the plains and creates such paradisiacal valleys as those seen in Kashmir *(left)*, beneath the Karakoram range.

Although the northern mountains are immense, they are cut toward the west by several passes, through which countless invaders and settlers over the centuries have clawed and picked their way. As a result, many of the people of the northland are descendants of tribes from Central Asia—among them Aryans and Huns—who brought new life and ideas to India over a period of 3,500 years.

A RAJASTHANI VILLAGER IN HIS BEST TURBAN

A TRIBE OF NOMADIC HERDSMEN

THE PLAINS: A NOMADIC LIFE WITH A KNIGHTLY PAST

To the southwest of the main mountain barrier sweep the high, dry plains of Rajasthan. Once this was the home of the warrior Rajput maharajahs, but today their power is gone and the land is little more than desert. The thick forests and tilled fields that dotted the plains were long ago felled by axes and overworked by plows in an attempt to feed expanding populations. Farmers still try to subsist, but most tribes now live a nomadic life, following their herds of cattle from one muddy watering hole to the next.

The great days of glory for the plains started in the Seventh Century, when the Rajputs, probably descendants of Central Asian tribes, controlled much of northern India. Their leaders divided the land into petty kingdoms, ruling them from turreted stone castles. These knightly horsemen had their own chivalry, and a passion for war. They rode forth regularly to fight each other, and later reluctantly united to defend Hinduism from the invading Muslims, who eventually overcame them. Today all that remains of the Rajputs is a romantic tradition, which lives on in ballads, legends and a memory of courtliness and military honor.

THE GANGES IN FLOOD DURING THE MONSOON

THE GANGES: A SACRED AND FERTILE HEARTLAND

India's spiritual home—which all Hindus long to visit at least once—is the Ganges River and the plains of the northeast through which it flows. Here crops are plentiful, for the rice and wheat fields are irrigated both by the river and by the seasonal monsoons, and the soil is rejuvenated with rich silt when monsoon rains make the Ganges overflow.

The Ganges is holy to the Hindus. A bath in its waters is thought to wash away all earthly sins; the cherished event of a lifetime is a pilgrimage to dip in the Ganges, at any one of the hundreds of holy sites that dot its course. Tributaries of the Ganges are also considered sacred. Along the Burhi Gandak River in Bihar Province *(above)*, parades of the faithful march to the water at sunset on the birthday of Dattatreya, one of the many Hindu deities. After placing offerings of food on the shore, each family sends one member into the river, where he is purified by the waters and by prayer.

25

THE DECCAN: A HARSH, STORM-SWEPT PLATEAU

HEAVY WINDS OVER THE SCRUBLAND NEAR MADRAS

Geographically, the heart of the huge peninsula forming southern India is the Deccan, a high, massive area that is diverse within itself, ranging from forests and arable fields to scrubland and mountains. Here, even more than in the Ganges basin, the monsoon dominates all life. Through each blistering spring, the soil is baked lifeless by the sun and desiccating winds, and the inhabitants move at a weary pace. Then, in early summer, just when the heat seems insupportable, the clouds that have been piling up in the distance burst open to disgorge torrential rains.

At first the monsoon is celebrated as a deliverance. Chil-

dren run through the heavy drops and young people dance in the downpour; the stifling heat is broken and the earth blooms in green profusion. But the land, baked hard as concrete, cannot absorb the rivers from the sky. Flash floods strike with sudden swiftness, often sweeping away and drowning scores of people in their muddy tides.

Not surprisingly, this land has long resisted settlement by newcomers. Those who live there are still largely Dravidians, who have occupied the Deccan since prehistoric times—a distinctive people who have tenaciously preserved their own ancient languages and literature for 2,000 years.

THE COAST: LINK TO THE WORLD

On the ocean side of the hills that fringe the Deccan plateau lie the tropical borders of southern India. The shoreline is often no more than five miles wide, but its wet climate and black soil support luxuriant sandalwood and teak forests, through which wild elephants roam. Here, too, rich spice plantations have long given substance to the legend of India's exotic produce. And from the palm-fringed beaches, fishing boats set out to net the fish that teem in the tropical waters.

For all its seeming tranquility, however, the Indian shoreline is not a hospitable one; there are few natural harbors and the tides offshore are often deceptive. The winds, so important for sailing ships, are totally dependent on the direction of the monsoons, which move toward the east in summer and the west in winter. Yet despite these hazards, southern India has for thousands of years been a gathering place for merchants. Traders from scores of countries have bartered at Indian ports of call, claiming not only spices, but also silks, ivory, gold and aromatics from all parts of India's varied land.

BRINGING PRODUCE TO MARKET ON A HOMEMADE RAFT

FISHING NETS AT COCHIN HARBOR

2

THE ROOTS OF
INDIAN CULTURE

A PROUD-VISAGED FIGURINE, *found in the ruins of Mohenjo Daro, is one of the few stone sculptures left from this once-thriving city. Archeologists think the figure, perhaps representing a priest, was used at a family altar.*

In Western history, a thousand years is a long time. The rise, decline and fall of the Roman Empire all took place within that span of time; ancient Greece rose and fell in less than half of it. But it took a full millennium—the years between about 1500 and about 500 B.C.—merely to lay the foundations of Hinduism. During those centuries, nomadic tribes from Central Asia overran the northern part of the Indian subcontinent. Borrowing from older cultures already on the land, they developed and enriched their own social and religious ideas. Though modified by reforms and evolutionary changes, these social and religious ideas still prevail in India: for modern Hindus, all the fundamental principles of society and religion were laid down in that first thousand years.

For nearly 2,000 years afterward, the period from 1500 to 500 B.C. was generally taken as the beginning of Indian history, for only in recent decades have men been able to peer further back into the Indian past. In some respects, recent discoveries leave the general picture unchanged; the birth of Hinduism is still the crucial starting point of historic India. But some of these discoveries are important and exciting for their own sake. They have extended our knowledge of Indian history by thousands of years, and they have turned up at least one great pre-Hindu civilization.

Archeologists and anthropologists now know that the beginnings of civilization in India are nearly as old as civilization itself. About 4000 B.C., soon after the appearance of farming communities in Mesopotamia, men in the northwest corner of India made the great transition from nomadic hunting and food-gathering to agriculture. West of the Indus River, on the hills of Baluchistan and the rim of the Iranian plateau, such men began to settle on the land. By 3000 B.C. they had developed a primitive village culture—a culture of farmers who lived in mud-and-wattle huts, and practiced the animistic worship of natural objects and forces.

Then, in a great and still-unexplained advance, these people developed one of the earliest of the world's great civilizations. Because the centers of this civilization were first found along the Indus River, some archeologists call it the Indus Valley civilization; others call it the Harappan Culture,

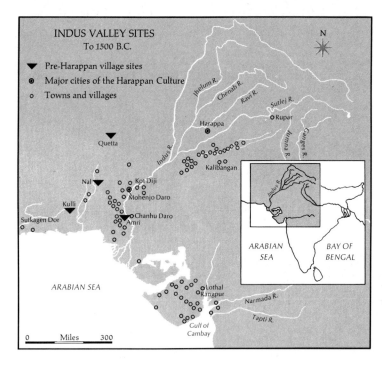

INDUS VALLEY SITES
To 1500 B.C.

▼ Pre-Harappan village sites
◎ Major cities of the Harappan Culture
○ Towns and villages

after one of its two capital cities. Whatever its name, it flourished mightily for a thousand years, from about 2500 to about 1500 B.C., and then mysteriously disappeared.

The discovery of the Harappan, or Indus Valley, civilization is one of the triumphs of modern archeology. Not until 1922, when an archeologist digging in what is now West Pakistan turned up a handful of bricks and stone seals, did anyone even guess at the civilization's existence. Since then hardly a year has passed without a significant find and an increase of knowledge, and the hunt for Harappan sites and artifacts is still underway. The story is still fragmentary, and important gaps remain to be filled. But the explorers have proved conclusively that the civilization was a great one, ranking with the other great river civilizations of its time—that of Egypt on the Nile, and of Sumer on the Tigris and Euphrates.

It was great, to begin with, in the sheer size of the territory it dominated—an extent of land far greater than that of Egypt or Sumer. The Harappan world covered a gigantic triangle with sides a thousand miles long. The apex of the triangle lay far up the Indus River system, or perhaps as far as the Ganges; its base extended along the coast from the head of the Arabian Sea, at the modern Iran-Pakistan border, to the Gulf of Cambay, near modern Bombay. Within this vast area archeologists have already found over 50 communities, ranging from farming towns and villages through large seaports to the two great capitals of the civilization—Mohenjo Daro, on the central Indus River, and Harappa, on a tributary about 400 miles to the northeast.

The diversity of these communities reflects the diversity of the Indus economy. To the farming communities came the produce of the countryside —wheat, barley, a variety of fruits and the earliest cultivated cotton in the world. The seaports were

magnificently equipped: the port of Lothal, on the Gulf of Cambay, contained an enclosed brick shipping dock over 700 feet long, controlled by a sluice gate and capable of loading ships at low and high tides. At such ports, Harappan traders dealt in gold and copper, turquoise and lapis lazuli, timber from the slopes of the Himalayas. Harappan ships sailed up the Persian Gulf to Mesopotamia, carrying Indian ivory and cotton to the age-old cities of Agade and Ur in the Tigris-Euphrates Valley. And all the wealth of farming, trading and shipping contributed to the wealth of the two capitals, the cities of Mohenjo Daro and Harappa.

Both capitals were masterpieces of urban planning. Each consisted essentially of a rectangle three miles in circumference, dominated by a fortified citadel as high as a modern five-story building. The citadel, containing a huge granary, a hall for ceremonial assemblies, and a public—perhaps ritualistic—bath, was apparently the center of government and religion. Below it, the city spread out in a rigidly mathematical gridiron pattern, with avenues and streets running north and south, east and west. Solidly built brick houses, shops and restaurants lined the streets, with windowless walls facing the streets themselves, entrances on narrow lanes behind the streets, and rooms graciously arranged around open interior courtyards. Even the sanitary arrangements in these buildings—the most elaborate in the world of that time—bespeak the sophistication of the Indus technology. Indoor baths and privies were connected by a system of drains and water chutes to sewers running beneath the main streets. At intervals, there were openings in the drains for the convenience of official inspectors. As the British archeologist Sir Mortimer Wheeler puts it, the planning and sanitary arrangements of the cities present a picture of "middle-class prosperity with zealous municipal controls."

In the arts, the people of these thriving cities excelled in brilliantly decorated wheel-turned pottery and small, beautifully executed figurines. There are pieces in terra cotta and glazed ceramic that apparently represent a "mother goddess," a seated male divinity, and a sacred bull and pipal tree. There are secular and even playful pieces, too: comic grotesques and caricatures; a coquettish bronze figure of a dancing girl, caught in mid-wiggle; and charming terra cotta toys—animals with jiggling heads, tiny ox carts pulled by strings.

As befitted a generally commercial culture, however, the richest store of Indus artifacts was apparently assembled by the merchant class, and for commercial ends. This store consists of soapstone seals, usually about an inch square, and probably designed to identify bales of cotton or bags of grain. Over a thousand such seals have been found at Mohenjo Daro alone; others have turned up as far away as the Persian Gulf and the cities of Mesopotamia. They provide at once an esthete's delight and an archeologist's puzzle. A delight, because they are exquisitely carved with figures of bulls, elephants, tigers, antelopes and other animal residents of the Indus Valley. A puzzle, because they almost invariably bear inscriptions in a delicate pictographic style—inscriptions that have obstinately defied all attempts at decipherment.

Because the seal inscriptions provide nearly all the surviving examples of Indus writing, they have been the objects of intense study. About 250 different pictographs have been identified—pictographs that are as different from Egyptian hieroglyphics and Mesopotamian cuneiform as these two ancient scripts are from each other—but the longest single inscription contains only 17 of these pictographic symbols. Lacking a key to the meanings of individual symbols, scientists can only speculate on this most tantalizing of all clues to the secrets of a civilization.

The seals are also part of another, larger puzzle: the disappearance of the Indus Valley civilization after about 1500 B.C. Toward the end of the thousand-year span of that civilization, the quality of the seals at Mohenjo Daro exhibits a curious decline. They are no longer made of stone, but of clay, and the lifelike engravings give way to crude geometric figures. Indeed, a decline takes place in every area of Mohenjo Daro's life. The pottery, once highly glazed and vividly colored, becomes plain and clumsy ware. Worst of all, the superb planning of the city collapses: the last buildings are mere higgledy-piggledy collections of jerry-built, shoddy hovels. In the end, the city is abandoned.

At Harappa the story is different, but equally baffling. There, archeologists have found no evidence of a slow decline: the life of the city seems simply to stop, while it is still in its maturity and at the height of its material prosperity. Such an ending, of course, is no less final than that of Mohenjo Daro; in the upper Indus Valley, as in the lower, the civilization completely disappeared.

Most archeologists agree that no single explanation can account for the disappearance of the Indus Valley civilization. A thousand years of farming, grazing and timbering may have so impoverished the land that it could no longer support a large and powerful civilization. Evidence of great floods at Mohenjo Daro suggests another explanation. Driven from the capital again and again, the people of Mohenjo Daro may have become homeless refugees elsewhere, and the lesser cities of the region may have declined for lack of leadership. Other geological changes, equally slow and irreversible, such as the lifting of an entire coastline, may have assaulted some cities even more directly: it is known, for example, that certain Indus seaports that once stood on the shore of the Arabian Sea now lie as much as 30 miles inland.

For the disappearance of the Indus culture in the north, these explanations will not suffice. There, the deathblow to the Indus civilization was sudden and violent. And the dealers of that deathblow, according to some historians, were tall, fair-skinned nomads from Central Asia, who swept into India's northwest plains about the middle of the Second Millennium B.C. Ravaging the country as they came, these nomads put an end to a culture far higher than their own. But they also set the course of all later Indian history.

The invaders called themselves Aryans—"the noble ones"—a word that may come from a long-dead Indo-European language. This language, which probably evolved as a number of closely related dialects, was spoken by great masses of barbarians who began to move out of the steppes of Central Asia about 2000 B.C. Some of these nomadic tribesmen settled in Asia Minor and Persia; others became the ancestors of the Greeks. The Aryans, who may have taken centuries to make their way into India, were probably typical of them all.

As they cut a swath through northwest India and eastward into the Punjab region, the Aryans introduced a pattern of life that was to persist for centuries. Intertribal warfare was common; temporary alliances were formed to conquer or subdue non-Aryan peoples. Some of these alliances must have been formed to attack the people of the Indus civilization. For such attacks, the Aryans flung

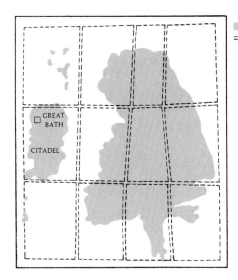

ARCHEOLOGICAL MOUNDS
PRINCIPAL STREETS

A MONUMENTAL BATH *is the most impressive structure yet excavated at Mohenjo Daro, a city of some 20,000 people that flourished in the Indus Valley between 2500 and 1500 B.C. Located in the citadel area of the city (map, above), the "Great Bath" was probably used mainly for religious rites, as is suggested by its arrangement of small ceremonial robing and bathing rooms (seen in the cutaway view at right). The rooms surround a courtyard containing a pool some 40 feet long and 8 feet deep, which was waterproofed with bitumen. Water from the pool emptied into a large vaulted drain more than 6 feet high (drawing below) that may have connected with the city's sewage system.*

DRAIN

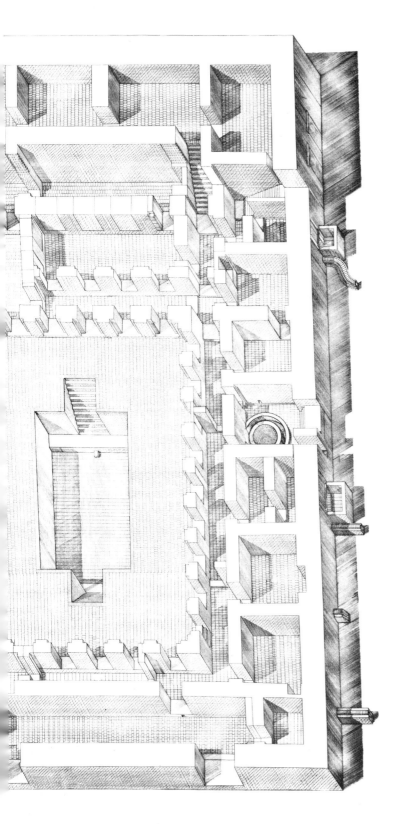

themselves into battle on light, swift, horse-drawn chariots—against a people who had never seen anything faster or more maneuverable than a lumbering bullock cart. Even the fortified citadels of the Indus cities succumbed to Aryan sieges and storms. In some of their earliest writings, the invaders described successful onslaughts against dark-skinned non-Aryan peoples who lived in *purs*, or "forts," and they called their war-god *puramdara*, "fort destroyer." Some archeologists identify one such fortified place, called Hari-Yupuya by the Aryans, as the great Indus city of Harappa.

Throughout the Indus Valley, the conquerors doomed the high urban civilization that preceded them. The Aryans were wandering herdsmen. Their food and clothing came from cattle; cows and bulls were their measure of wealth; and though they eventually took to farming they continued to feel that a man's dignity lay in his herds rather than in his crops. Such a people could not maintain or even comprehend a complex urban culture. Writing, craftsmanship, arts and architecture—these ornaments and achievements of the Indus civilization died in Aryan hands.

For this reason, the early Aryan period is a sort of archeologist's nightmare. The Aryans left no cities and statues, no stone seals, no pots or bricks or cemeteries for scientists to dig up, classify and interpret. What they did leave, however, is one of the most extraordinary bodies of literature in all the world. The great "artifact" of the Aryan culture—and, in fact, very nearly the sole source of information about Aryan history and society during that period—is a collection of religious writings, a set of scriptures.

In India, Aryan priests built up an exhaustive record of their religious beliefs and practices. Composed in a complex poetic style already perfected in pre-Indian days, and passed along by memorization and recitation, this record grew by slow accretion for a thousand years. Its four great books, the Vedas, have given their name to that entire period of Indian history. The years from 1500 to 500 B.C. —the thousand-year period in which the fundamental principles of Hinduism were laid down— are generally called the Vedic Age.

The earliest and most important of the four Vedic books, the Rig Veda, consists of over a thousand hymns—a heterogeneous collection of prayers, instructions for rituals, incantations, poems on nature, and such secular songs as a gambler's lament over his luck at dice. The other three books, more specialized in content, are the Yajur Veda, the Sama Veda and the Atharva Veda, which consist respectively of technical instructions for the priests, ritual formulas and magical spells.

During the long Vedic Age, commentaries on the Vedas—and commentaries on these commentaries —were gradually compiled. The Brahmanas, commentaries on the Vedas themselves, discuss specific techniques of rituals in enormous detail. The Aranyakas, or "forest books," deal with the language of the rituals—phrases, words, syllables, even individual sounds. And in the Upanishads, a collection of philosophical treatises, the main concern is with the mystical significance of ritual rather than its practice: the Upanishads expound a multitude of speculative interpretations of the universe and man's place in it.

Just as the lack of concrete Aryan remains has frustrated the archeologist, the Vedas and their voluminous commentaries have baffled the historian. Other sacred literatures, including the Bible, often deal with sequences of events in time. The ancient Hebrews, for example, might tell the story of a particular king's defeat in battle because the story revealed something about the way in which God operated in the world. The Vedas, on the other hand, never treat historical events as manifestations of the Aryan gods. For the authors

of the Vedas, ritual formed the only direct connection between man and the gods. As a result, the Vedas provide no dates, no dynasties, no wars or peace treaties—no events or series of events that a historian can place in any precise chronology.

The oldest sacred books do, however, reveal a great deal about the Aryan religion and society, and later books reveal how that religion and society slowly changed during the thousand years of the Vedic Age.

We know, for example, that the religion brought to India by the Aryans was, as might be expected, a cult of gods related to the needs of a more northern life—gods of fire, of warming drink and sheer ferocity. We know, too, that these gods were served by a separate priesthood, who performed sacrificial rituals. Indeed, the rite of sacrifice lay at the heart of early Aryan religion. No temples or images were involved: the rite was performed at a simple open altar, where a sacred fire carried to the gods the food and drink that men themselves enjoyed —cooked grain, slaughtered animals, clarified butter and an intoxicating potion called "soma."

Soma itself was one of the Aryan gods. For its preparation, a certain plant, now unknown, was pressed between stones and its juice was mixed with milk. Drunk during the ritual, it induced in the celebrants hallucinations, such as the illusion of enormous size. Until recent studies of psychedelic drugs, historians were at a loss to explain how soma, an unfermented drink, could cause intoxication in those who used it. It now seems likely that the sacred drink was actually a "mind-expanding" antique LSD.

The sacred fire, too, was a god. Agni, the god of fire, had a curious variety of functions and jurisdictions. "Butter-backed and flame-haired," according to the Rig Veda, he lived in three places: on earth, in heaven and throughout the air between. On earth, the sacred fire became the mouth with which the gods consumed burnt offerings. In heaven, Agni was the sun. And in the air he was the lightning, carrying messages up to the gods or bringing the gods down to earth when they were summoned in the rituals.

More human in his characteristics than either Soma or Agni was Indra, the god of heroes and of war, who led the Aryans in battle and used a thunderbolt as a weapon. Pleasure-loving and quite amoral, Indra was a perfect counterpart for the cheerful optimists who worshiped him. (He may, in fact, have been a deification of some early Aryan leader.) His fondness for feasting and drinking, gambling and dancing—and, of course, for making war—reflected the character of a robust, extroverted people who had little of the spirituality and none of the pessimism that are now commonly associated with India.

Among these people, the great cohesive force was not the rule of the gods, but the basic idea of an all-pervading cosmic order called "rita." Rita was the law that both sustained the universe and regulated the conduct of men. It governed such rhythms as those of day and night, or the turning of the seasons, and it fixed the relationships of man to the gods and of a man to other men. Thus, for the Aryans, men were part of the law of nature. If men lied or were carried away by anger or drink, they disturbed the cosmic order.

Rita itself was associated with a god—Varuna, an awesome, unyielding figure who sat in a palace in heaven. Varuna had not created the cosmic order; he was merely its guardian. But he guarded rita so sternly that he became the only god that the Aryans really feared.

Certainly, there was little else they feared. The Vedas picture a people of enormous pride, utterly convinced of their own racial and social superiority. For the local peoples of India, the non-Aryans, they had nothing but contempt and overwhelming scorn. These conquered peoples were completely segregated, forced to live in clusters outside the Aryan village boundaries and banned from Aryan religious rites.

The principle of segregating the non-Aryans also extended to the social order. According to the Vedas, the Aryans came into India loosely divided into three classes. At the top of each tribe were hereditary nobles, who chose one of their number as chief, or raja (an Indo-European word related to the Latin *rex*, or "king"). The second class consisted of priests, responsible for religious teaching and observances. Then came the ordinary tribesmen, the tenders of cattle. All conquered peoples were herded into a fourth group—a group that was inferior to the other three.

This early class system was not the caste system of modern India; there were, for example, no restrictions on diet or dining practices, on marriage or on hereditary occupation. "A bard [professional poet] am I, my father is a leech [physician] and my mother grinds corn," wrote an anonymous Aryan of the time. Nevertheless, the function of each class and of each member of a class was perfectly clear and distinct. A raja, for instance, probably owned more cattle than any other noble, but his role was simply that of a member of the noble class. He was not considered divine, nor was he a priest-king. The closest he could come to playing a religious role was to request sacrifices for the good of the tribe. Only the priests, a separate class, could perform such sacrifices.

Such were the social and religious patterns of early Aryan life. During the thousand-year course of the Vedic Age, however, these patterns gradually evolved into different ones, more complex and more rigid. The great force behind this evolution was the same one that had brought Aryans to India in the first place: the constant movement, century after century, of the Aryan people.

Some time after they had learned enough about agriculture to grow crops of their own, the Aryans began to move deeper into India. From their first base, the Indus Valley and the Punjab, their route ran southeast to the middle of the Indo-Gangetic plain, the area of modern Delhi. From there, they probably conquered and colonized their way to the Ganges itself, then followed the river southward to settle the area around Banaras (newly restored to its ancient name, Varanasi). The movement was a gradual one. As many as 600 years probably passed before the Aryans began to penetrate the Deccan.

During this long period of territorial expansion, Aryan tribes fought continually against each other and, more important, against the original inhabitants of the land. Among these indigenous peoples, two groups—the Panis and the Dasas—loom out of the mists of Vedic history. The Panis may have been aboriginal peoples of the very earliest hill cultures in the northwest. Apparently, they offered little resistance to the Aryan advance; for the most part, they appear dimly in the Vedic writings as robbers who stole cattle and had to be punished. Far more formidable—and even more difficult to identify—were the Dasas. They may have been remnants or relatives of the peoples of the Indus civilization; some historians suggest that they were Dravidians, the people of southern India. In any case, they proved far less easy to handle than the Panis. At one time the Dasas raised 10,000 men to oppose the Aryans, but were defeated. As always, the Aryans treated their enemy with complete contempt. In the Vedas, the Dasas are described as "evil-tongued" and "flat-nosed," and in the Aryans' Sanskrit language the very word *dasa* ultimately came to mean "slave."

The conquest of new lands and contacts with new peoples combined to bring profound changes to the Aryan way of life. Wandering tribes settled in small kingdoms; the tribal chiefs, once chosen by their peers, became power-hungry hereditary kings ruling from permanent capitals. And as kingdoms grew in territory and population, and victors and vanquished fused, the loose classes of Aryan society became more complex.

In the later Vedic Age, a king's realm usually included conquered Aryan tribes and a number of non-Aryan villages. To meet the threat of revolt, and of attacks from outside the kingdom, kings recruited standing armies from the old noble class of warriors. The kings themselves now claimed a rank far above that of other nobles.

The old class of ordinary tribesmen—once the herdsmen among the original nomadic Aryans— became peaceful farmers, cattle breeders, artisans and tradesmen. Meanwhile, descendants of the non-Aryan peoples became a fourth class—a class of laborers, who did the drudgery that freed higher classes for their occupations and interests.

The greatest change of all took place among the priests—a change not so much of function as of status. In early Aryan society, the priest class had held the second rank, below the nobles. Now they raised themselves above the nobles, above the kings —even above the gods. They accomplished this feat by giving a new importance—indeed, a new meaning—to religious ritual.

Over the years, the priests had developed enormously complex rituals out of the relatively simple ceremonies of the Rig Veda. In addition, they emphasized the idea that if a ritual were performed incorrectly catastrophe would ensue. If a single brick of the altar were out of line by a hair's breadth, if the sacrificial goat were touched at the wrong spot, then the cosmic order called rita would be upset and chaos would come.

This demand for ritual accuracy may have helped to improve the priests' skill at altar building and their knowledge of anatomy. What was far more important, it exalted the priesthood. Rita depended more upon the correct performance of rituals than upon the gods for whom rituals were performed. The gods merely guarded rita; the rituals actually affected it. And since only the priests could perform these rituals, the priests held the final responsibility for cosmic order. They were the most important creatures in the universe.

Even the kings assented to the glorification of the priesthood. The Rig Veda assured them that "that king, indeed, overpowers all opposing forces . . . who maintains [the priest] well attended, and praises and honors him as a deity." In turn, the priests gave religious support to the rajas and their expanding kingdoms. At times, that support resulted in curious combinations of piety and power politics. A case in point was the ritual of the "horse sacrifice."

In preparation for the horse sacrifice, a beautiful stallion was consecrated and allowed to wander for a full year. All the territory the stallion entered was claimed for the king who had commissioned the ritual. A band of armed warriors attended the horse, and the kings of usurped lands had to give up their property or fight for it. Finally, the horse was gently herded home and sacrificed in elaborate ceremonies involving hundreds of priests.

Along with the new interdependence of king and priest, there was a new religious justification for the class system. In one of the later Vedic writings, the priests proclaimed that the universe had been born when the gods sacrificed an Ideal Man or World Spirit and created classes of men from parts of his body. A Vedic hymn asks how social classes were created, and, in the answers, gives religious sanction to the four divisions of Aryan society:

> When they [the gods] divided the Man,
> into how many parts did they divide him?
> What was his mouth, what were his arms,
> what were his thighs and his feet called?

AN ANCIENT TREE OF LANGUAGE

The Sanskrit characters above may look utterly remote from anything Western, but in fact Sanskrit, the classical language of India, is related to almost all the languages of Europe, including English. The word is "Arya," or "Aryan," the name of the people who began to conquer India about 1500 B.C. Most ancient Indian literature was written in the Aryan tongue, Sanskrit, and Hindi, modern India's national language, is written in characters that are derived from it.

Sanskrit is a branch of a linguistic tree known as Indo-European. The trunk of the tree was a common tongue probably spoken in the region northwest of the Black Sea about 2500 B.C. After the people living in this region migrated in different directions, the tree branched into different but related languages. "Iran," the modern name for Persia, for example, resembles the Sanskrit "Arya." In Celtic the word was transformed into "Erin," which in English became "Ireland." Other examples of word relationships:

Pitar, the Sanskrit word for "father," is a close cognate of the Latin pater, the German Vater and the English words "father" and "paternal."

Ayas, meaning "metal" in Sanskrit, comes from the same root word as the Latin aes (bronze), the German Eisen (iron) and the English "iron."

The Sanskrit iras, or "anger," bears a close resemblance to the Latin ira, which became "ire" in English and appears in words like "irritable."

The Indo-European word pets (foot) became pat in Sanskrit and pes in Latin, and appears in such English words as "pedal" and "pedestrian."

Satam, the Sanskrit word for "one hundred," is a cousin of the Latin centum, which lives on in English words like "century" and "centennial."

The brahman [priest] was his mouth,
of his arms was made the warrior,
his thighs became the vaishya [farmer
    or merchant],
of his feet the shudra [servant] was born.

The implications of this primal sacrifice went far beyond the idea of social classes. Every time the priests performed their rites, they mystically repeated the creation of the world; the cosmic order died and was born again. And the death and rebirth of the universe implied the death and rebirth of every living thing in the universe. What is more, it implied a continuous cycle of such deaths and rebirths.

For human beings, this cycle of death and rebirth meant reincarnation, one of the basic concepts of Hinduism. In the earliest statements of the doctrine, reincarnation involved a great deal of traveling on the part of the soul. If a man lived a good life, his soul passed after death to the paradise of the gods. From there it went to the moon, from the moon to empty space, and it then descended to earth again in the form of rain. On earth, in the words of the Upanishads, souls "become food . . . and are offered again in the altar-fire which is man, to be born again in the fire of woman."

The entire journey, though, depended upon whether a man had lived a good or bad life. Only the man who had devoted himself to good pursuits —charity, sacrifice and austerity—would be rewarded by rebirth in a human body. The unrighteous would be reborn as worms, birds or insects. Thus, it was a man's conduct in this life that determined whether his status would rise or fall in future lives, and whether he would be happy or miserable. The Hindu concept of "karma" was slowly being born, and, along with that essentially theological concept, Hinduism's justification for extreme and irremediable inequalities in human society.

Clearly, a thousand years of development and change had brought the Aryans a long way from their beginnings. The purely Aryan tribal life of the early Vedic Age had given way to a complex social order and an advanced religion. The contrasts between the beginning and the end of the age can be briefly summarized.

The Aryans had come to India with simple, direct feelings for men and for the gods. In return for an offering of food or drink poured into a fire at a hearth, men received the blessings of the gods. Girls chose their husbands freely, and shifts of class membership were not impossible. Family life was open and informal, and the patriarchal family way of life was duplicated in tribal life. The chief, like the father of a family, had authority but not absolute authority. His power was subject to common law and Aryan traditions, which he could not override.

A thousand years later, the kings in their palaces were arrogant, ambitious rulers, most of them determined to rule the world. The old, easy family life was overlaid and formalized by religious ideas of divinely ordained hereditary classes, and by a host of restrictions and proscriptions. Religion itself had become two very different things: on the one hand, a great complex of meticulously organized rites; on the other, an intellectual discipline beyond the comprehension of most ordinary people. And priests were by far the most powerful group in the community.

In effect, Hinduism had come into existence. Toward the end of the Vedic Age dramatic protests were to be made against it by such men as Gautama Buddha, the greatest of all Indian religious leaders, but such protests did not alter the fundamentals of Indian religion or society. The Aryan-fostered, priest-led way of life had been securely founded, and would prevail through all the rest of the subcontinent's history.

A PROUD BULL, *among the earliest animals venerated by Indians, adorns a 4,000-year-old stone carving.*

ANIMALS BELOVED AND REVERED

Throughout their long history the diverse peoples of India have shared a fascination with, and respect for, animals. Cattle have always been held in particularly high regard: by the prehistoric Indus Valley tribes, which left hundreds of seals like the one above, bearing meticulously worked carvings of bulls; by the later Aryan herdsmen, who considered cattle the basic unit of wealth and used them as currency; and by the Hindus, who forbid killing them even now.

This attitude went far beyond respect for the usefulness of animals. Hindus, Buddhists and Jains regarded all forms of life as equally important, considering them incarnations of a single energy or life force. They believed that when a creature died this energy was reincarnated in some other form. Killing a living thing was thus unthinkable, because even an insect might be vitalized by the soul of an ancestor or friend. On a still higher plane, Hindu mythology endowed the gods with animal attributes. Even the 16th Century Muslim conquerors of northern India were captivated by this attitude toward animals, and commissioned some of the finest representations of them in Indian art.

BIRDS: NATIVE, EXOTIC AND MYTHICAL

To the ancient Indians, as to other early peoples, birds soaring into the sky were a source of inspiration. They associated them with another denizen of the heavens—the sun, in India a searing force, ruthlessly drying up the land until the arrival of the blessed monsoon rains. As Hinduism developed, the sun's power was represented as a mythological half-bird, half-man called Garuda *(right)*, while the principle of water was symbolized by sinuously curving serpents.

Real, as well as mythical, birds figured in traditional Indian life. The Indus Valley people left numerous representations of native birds, such as chickens and doves. Thousands of years later, the Muslim emperors of India were so intrigued by birds from far-off lands that they kept unusual varieties in aviaries and had their painters portray them realistically for court albums.

A TERRA-COTTA HEN, *found in the Indus Valley, was probably used as a child's whistle. Many clay toys have been unearthed in the valley, most in the form of birds and other animals.*

THE BIRDLIKE SUN PRINCIPLE, *Garuda, is shown in this painting bearing Indian gods on his back. Since Garuda was known as a devourer of serpents, snakebite victims appeal to him.*

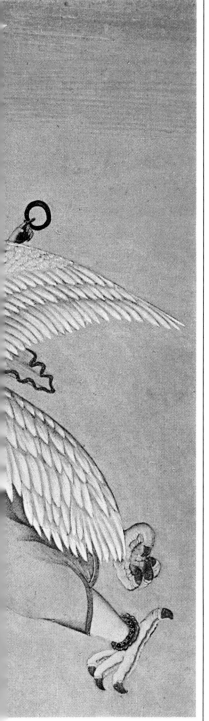

A TREE OF LIFE *represents creative forces in the universe. Sunbirds sit on the branches; a five-headed cobra, symbolizing water, rises from the trunk.*

A SPLENDID TURKEY *was imported by a Muslim emperor, Jahangir, who was keenly interested in nature and commissioned many studies of birds, animals and plants.*

MONKEYS: WISE ALLIES OF GODS AND MEN

According to an ancient Hindu myth, an army of monkeys once helped the legendary hero Rama rescue his wife from the demon Ravana. Since Rama was an incarnation of the god Vishnu, monkeys have been honored ever since. They also play significant roles in less-exalted fables; these tales, in which animals think and talk like people to make a moral point, were part of the education of every young Indian boy of noble birth.

One such story, illustrating the perils of listening to spiteful talk, tells of a monkey and a crocodile who were great friends. The crocodile's wife, however, became jealous and demanded the monkey's heart, and so the crocodile tricked the monkey into climbing on his back and then tried to drown him. But the monkey convinced the crocodile that he had a better heart stored in a tree in the forest. The crocodile carried the monkey back to shore, only to discover that he had been twice deceived, and had lost his best friend.

A PENSIVE MONKEY *is one member of a group of life-sized animal figures carved into a huge boulder at a sacred place of worship on India's southeastern coast.*

A CAPTIVE MONKEY *on a tether may have been a nobleman's pet, or one of many animals that India's rajas kept in menageries.*

MONKEYS AT PLAY—*fishing, eating, quarreling and climbing trees—
are shown in this delightful 16th Century painting, which was
used to illustrate a book of fables, "The Lights of Canopus."* 45

THE UBIQUITOUS COW: A BASIC SOURCE OF LIFE

For countless centuries cattle have been the most essential animals in India. Bullocks served as draft animals and chronically inadequate food supplies made cows' milk a basic food. Their droppings have long been the only fuel in most Indian households, because of a perennial shortage of wood.

To the Hindu, veneration of the cow is an inseparable part of life, rooted in deep tradition. Yet cows are not truly sacred; the Hindu religion merely prohibits killing them. They also represent the pastoral life, which is considered idyllic. The god Krishna, creator of the universe, grew up among cattle and cowherds, and the story of his childhood with them is a favorite Hindu tale *(pages 123-133)*. To Hindus the bull, rather than the cow, was sacred. Symbols of procreation since prehistoric times, bulls were also associated with the god Shiva, and were carved at his temples.

A WHITE-FACED COW, *garlanded with bells, climbs out of the river and prepares to graze on a flowered bank. The picture is a detail from a painting illustrating the boyhood of Krishna.*

A DOCILE HERD *of cows and nursing calves is depicted on a cotton wall-hanging. Entitled the "Paradise of Krishna," the scene represents a traditional Indian conception of pastoral peace.*

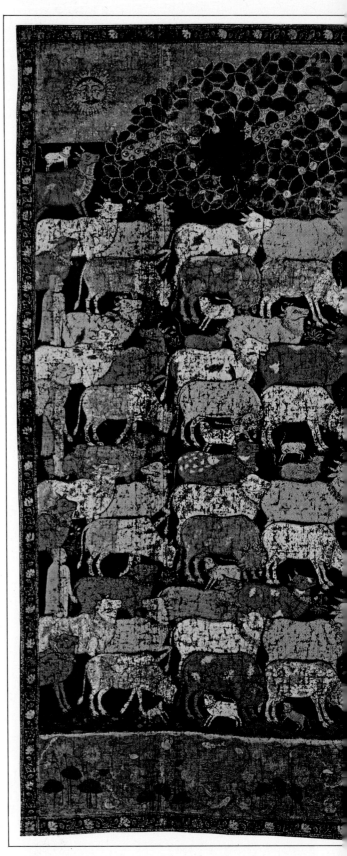

A MONUMENTAL BULL (above) was carved in the Third Century B.C. It stood on a column built by Emperor Ashoka, which was inscribed with Buddhist edicts.

A HUMPED BULL, surrounded by peacocks, is shown on a decorative Mughal plate (at right). Although Muslims did not accept the symbolic meaning of cattle, they used them as artistic motifs.

ELEPHANTS: BRINGERS OF RAIN AND GOOD LUCK

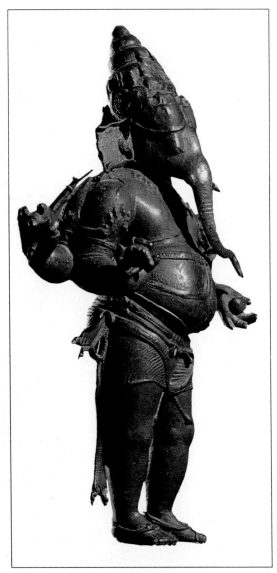

According to Hindu mythology, the first elephants in the world had wings and consorted with the clouds. One day, however, a group of elephants alighted on a branch under which an ascetic saint was teaching his pupils. Not surprisingly, the branch broke and fell on the pupils, killing several of them and enraging the saint, who called on the gods to deprive the elephants of their wings. But the elephants remained friendly with the clouds, and it was still in their power to call upon their former heavenly companions to bring rain. For this blessed ability elephants are still honored in India. Particularly revered are the pure white elephants traditionally kept by kings, who consider the discovery of one of these rare specimens to be an omen of good fortune. Worshiping them is associated with rainfall and bountiful crops. Even today the symbol of good luck is an elephant-headed divinity called Ganesha, to whom Hindus pray before every important undertaking.

GOD OF GOOD LUCK, *the elephant-headed divinity Ganesha is traditionally shown with a fat belly, symbolizing the prosperity that he brings to those who worship him.*

A BABY ELEPHANT, *struggling to stand upright at the feet of its mother, was carved in stone at Mamallapuram, a sacred Indian site.*

PLAYFUL ELEPHANTS—*wallowing in the lotus pool, dancing on the shore—are depicted under a blazing sky before the monsoon.*

3

A SEARCH FOR ENLIGHTENMENT

By an odd coincidence in history, the Sixth Century B.C. was a century of remarkable intellectual discovery for nearly every ancient civilization. In Israel the prophet Jeremiah was urging on his people a deep sense of individual responsibility for their destiny. In Greece the philosopher Anaximander was proposing that all forms of life arose from a single source, and Heraclitus was asserting that the basic feature of life was impermanence. In China the great Confucius was preaching a code of ethical behavior similar to the Biblical Golden Rule. In Persia Zarathustra asserted that humankind faced a choice between truth and evil—a choice that "each man [must decide] for his own self."

Everywhere that man had developed a complex culture, human thought was rising to higher levels of abstraction, reaching new conceptions of the universe, clarifying the human role in the world order, and formulating durable religious beliefs. India, no less than other lands, was in a state of intellectual ferment. Indian philosophers addressed themselves to the same questions that caught the imaginations of men in Israel, Greece, China and Persia. The answers they found in the Sixth Century B.C. made India a center of religious creativity. They drew on an existing body of sacred teachings, but they went beyond these to found an important heterodox sect, Jainism, and a religion of world importance, Buddhism, both of which interacted with the older religion of the brahman priests to catalyze the development of the Hindu religion. In so doing they transformed India from a country primarily given to the worship of natural forces and magic ritual to a nation justly famed for its concern with deep religious understanding.

Perhaps so many stimulating ideas arose simultaneously in these far-flung lands because men communicated with one another through trade; perhaps the coinciding of genius was due solely to chance. The historical facts can probably never be known, much less the causes. Changing social and economic conditions may have played a role in all these places. In a good many parts of Sixth Century India trade and agriculture were thriving, cities were growing, large kingdoms were superseding the rule of old tribal families. The rise of commerce brought a higher standard of living, and with it,

A DEVOUT PILGRIM *worships at the huge, flower-strewn feet of a statue of Gommatesvara, one of the Jain sect's major saints. Since the Sixth Century B.C., followers of this religion have taught ascetic self-denial.*

time to think. Such a shift in social structure generally brings alienation as well; with old supports gone and old values coming to seem irrelevant, new ones have to be found.

Even before the Sixth Century B.C. men of India had demonstrated a philosophical bent. Their earliest religious scripture, the Rig Veda, appeared sometime in the Second Millennium B.C. This consisted chiefly of hymns to a host of deities—the war-god, the fire-god; animistic spirits of sky, sun and moon, of rivers and storms, of animals and trees. Some of the Vedic hymns, however, expressed a spirit of philosophical inquiry. One of them, after listing a host of deities, asked: "Whom, then, shall we honor with our sacrifices?"

After the composition of the Rig Veda, Indian philosophers began to compose commentaries on the hymns, a practice they continued for hundreds of years. The final and most significant portion of the resulting literature is a collection of philosophical speculations. This portion, begun about 700 B.C. and called the Upanishads, contained many of the themes that inspired the originators of Jainism and Buddhism and provided the religious foundation for Hinduism. The name comes from two Sanskrit words, *upa*, meaning "near," and *shad*, "to sit," because the Upanishads, developed before writing was common in India, were passed on orally by sages to pupils sitting nearby.

The Upanishads probe into the nature of the universe and the human soul, and the relation of each to the other. They make no absolute statements of right and wrong, of creation, the gods or man; instead they speculate, seeking always to find truth, as opposed to stating it, and offering a wide range of possibilities. But the Upanishads set the tone for all further religious development in India, and in this they are the most sacred of literature.

"Whence are we born, where do we live, and whither do we go?" the Upanishads asked. In

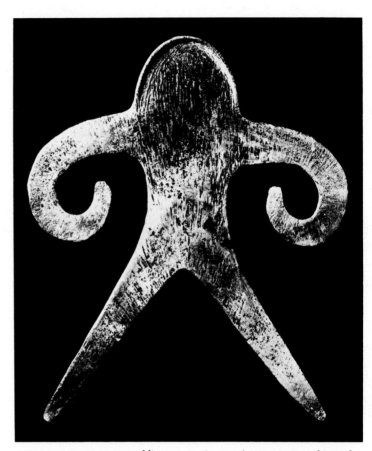

A MYSTERIOUS FIGURE, *resembling a man, is one of many copper objects dating from about 1000 B.C. that have been found on the Gangetic plain and connected to the Vedic religion that thrived there. The use of this piece is not known, but a similar one was found imbedded in a sacrificial altar.*

searching for answers to these questions about the nature of the universe, they did not forsake ancient beliefs. They accepted the many gods of the ancient Vedic pantheon, but they sought to find unity in the multiplicity of the world around them. In that effort they developed the idea that all the gods, all people, all the many aspects of the universe devolved from a single world spirit—and that spirit, which they called Brahman, resided in all the forms that proceeded from it.

Brahman cannot be precisely defined; the Upanishads described the spirit only in general terms as the Divine Essence "hidden in all beings, all-pervading, the self within all beings, watching over all works, dwelling in all beings, the witness, the perceiver. . . . He is the one ruler . . . he makes the one seed manifold."

Despite their recognition of an all-encompassing being, the Upanishads continued to praise the many ancient gods, and in this the Indians remained polytheistic. But in the effort to find unity in multiplicity, to find one pervasive spirit that abided everywhere, they moved toward monism—not monotheism, the Judaic concept that says "There is one God," but a belief that all gods, all people and all things are merely different manifestations of one spirit that pervades the universe. In this view they related the whole of the universe to each man's "self" or soul, the Atman.

As Brahman cannot be defined, neither can the Atman. It exists, but it cannot be captured; life proceeds from it, yet it has no tangible quality. This idea is expressed in a famous parable:

"Fetch me a fruit from the banyan tree," said Svetaketu's father to his son.
"Here is a fruit, sir."
"Break it."
"I have broken it, sir."
"What do you see?"
"Very tiny seeds, sir."

"Break one."
"I have broken it, sir."
"Now what do you see?"
"Why, nothing, sir."
"Dear son, what you do not see is the essence of the banyan tree. In that essence the mighty banyan tree exists. The essence, my dear, is the unseen spirit which pervades everywhere. It is the Self of all things. And you are that Self, Svetaketu."

"You are that Self"—you are one with the spirit that pervades the universe—is the meaning of monism and the predominant theme of Indian religions.

Elsewhere in the Upanishads the connection between individuality and Brahman is expressed in another image. "As flowing rivers disappear in the sea, losing their name and form, thus a wise man, freed from name and form, goes to the divine person who is beyond all."

This idea lies at the opposite pole from one of the major themes of Western thought, which extols the individual above all else. But the absorption of individuality in a greater whole was—and is—the Indian idea of bliss. The Upanishads say, "When to a man who understands, the Self has become all things, what sorrow, what trouble, can there be to him who once beheld that unity?"

Until man achieves that understanding, the Upanishads explain, he must endure repeated rebirths. The existence of his Atman has nothing whatever to do with the body in which it happens to reside at a given time. The body is like a suit of clothes the soul wears; as a suit of clothes is shed when it is worn out, so the soul sheds a worn-out body and puts on a new one.

The process of putting on a new body, shedding it at the appropriate time, then putting on still another one—the cycle of reincarnation or transmigration of the soul—is one of three fundamental ideas of Indian thought. The "clothes" of the soul may be subhuman creatures—insects and animals. But not until a human body clothes the soul does it become conscious, responsible for its behavior and hence for progress toward its birth in a higher state. Then it can strive for the ultimate goal, awareness of its unity with the universe.

The progress of the soul is regulated by karma, the law of cause and effect that is the second key Indian concept. Because of karma, a good act reaps a good result and an evil act reaps a bad result; a good life will lead to rebirth in a better life in the next reincarnation, but a bad one will merit return to a lower order. Karma, then, is not unlike the Biblical maxim "Whatsoever a man soweth, that shall he also reap." Each man's condition in life— his tranquillity or misery, his mental scope, his social standing—is a direct and unavoidable result of his particular karma, of the good or evil acts he performed in his previous life. In the same manner his next life will depend on the karma set by the way he thinks and acts in the present one.

The doctrine of karma sanctifies the status quo, making things as they are seem inevitable. By enshrining traditional ways, it stifles innovation, supports the rigid segregation of the caste system and excuses social injustice. Nevertheless, it also imbues Indian life with inextinguishable hope and ambition for personal improvement. The lowliest man may look forward to a better lot in the next life if he lives this one well. Indeed he is driven toward righteousness by the knowledge that his actions determine his condition.

To help the Indian advance in his cycle of rebirths, he has a third concept that interacts with the other two: that is dharma, the duty by which he is bound, according to his present station in life. If he abides by his dharma, acting out his life as duty stipulates, his karma will be good; if his karma is good, his rebirth in a good life the next time around will be his reward.

The three concepts of a cycle of rebirth, an im-mutable karma and a duty-bound dharma, all leading to the ultimate goal of absorption in the universal spirit, had by the Sixth Century B.C. formed the foundation of Indian belief. It was an enduring foundation, and it remains the support of several distinct religions to this day. But it was not the only contribution of the Upanishads.

While the Upanishads were expounding basic ideas they were also transforming man's view of himself. This resultant reassessment of the human estate may be their most significant achievement.

In the earliest Vedic writings, the gods had been paramount. Religion had been concerned primarily with sacrifice—the consuming of animals and food by sacred fire, which carried the offerings up to the gods, and the utterance of magic formulas. But in proposing that the human soul is one with the Supreme Spirit, the brahman priests who composed the Upanishads had in effect deified mankind.

That idea had far-reaching consequences. By the middle of the Sixth Century, other men besides the brahmans had begun to engage in philosophical exploration. When they did, they built on the foundations laid in the Upanishads, but many of them challenged the intellectual and religious rule of the brahmans. Some turned hedonistic and preached a philosophy of worldly enjoyment; others sought an explanation of life in asceticism and contemplation. Among them they spawned a plethora of cults that either openly challenged the brahmans and their ritual, or went their own way quietly.

The hedonists were far outnumbered by the ascetics. These men left their families, friends and all their possessions and retired to peaceful forests, where they devoted themselves exclusively to spiritual meditation. They aimed at rendering themselves oblivious to sensation, that they might find inner peace in their withdrawal from the world.

Some of the ascetics were so avid to free themselves of all worldly interference that they spent most of their energies on bizarre, even psychotic, exercises—such feats of self-mortification as sitting near a blazing fire in the broiling sun, walking on nails or holding one hand above the head until the arm atrophied. Not all ascetics indulged in practices quite so extreme as these; the more moderate among them learned to sit motionless for hours, immune to the stimuli of the physical world, so that they could concentrate on mental exploration. They turned their complete attention inward, going, as the Upanishads put it, "from darkness to darkness deeper yet," seeking always to solve the mystery of man and the universe.

By a combination of intense thinking and mystic concentration, many ascetics enabled their minds to roam with rarely attainable freedom, sometimes so successfully that they came upon fresh and valuable insights. When they did reach new theories about the meaning of life, they were eager to share their discoveries with others. Numbers of them then left their forest retreats and wandered through the countryside, preaching to all who would listen. Apparently there were many people ready to listen to new philosophical ideas in Sixth Century India. Hundreds of the ascetics acquired followers and heterodox cults proliferated throughout the land.

Some of the cults were antibrahman; a few seem to have been antireligious. "When the body dies," said the leader of one such cult, denying both rebirth and karma, "both fool and wise alike are cut off and perish." Most of the cults seem to have flourished briefly and disappeared. Out of hundreds, perhaps thousands, of cults that arose, two survived to alter brahman tradition and endure as independent, significant sects. They were Jainism and Buddhism.

The founder of Jainism was a youth named Var-

dhamana. If he had been born in medieval Europe, he might well have been a "verray parfit gentil knight" such as the one described by Chaucer. He was born about 540 B.C. into a setting of wealth, nobility and pride. His father was an Indian lord, a powerful chieftain of the Jnatrika clan that lived south of Nepal. Vardhamana seems to have been drawn to asceticism early in his life, but to have resisted the call and lived in the manner of his aristocratic family until he was 30, when his parents died. Then he left his home and all his worldly possessions to become a mendicant. From the start he practiced extreme austerities. He set out wearing one thin garment; after 13 months, he discarded even that, and went for the rest of his life "sky-clad"—naked.

He devoted 12 years to austerity, debate with other wanderers and meditation, and finally he reached the goal of all ascetics: an instant of perceiving the meaning of life and death. Then he set about sharing his enlightenment with others. So persuasive was he that disciples quickly rallied to him, calling him Mahavira, the "Great Hero," and Jina, the "Conqueror." From that word came the name of his cult, Jainism—"Religion of the Conquerors."

Like many of the reformers of medieval Christianity some two thousand years after him, Mahavira accepted without quarrel the fundamental principles of established doctrine, but challenged the ruling hierarchy. Mahavira accepted karma and reincarnation and the concepts of Atman and Brahman, but he provided new interpretations of the ideas. Previously karma, for instance, had been an abstract principle; Mahavira likened it to material substance. He taught that karma consisted of impurities that clung to the soul like spiritual barnacles. Everything had a soul—not only man and animals, but trees, rivers, even stones as well. The soul of man was clear and pure at first,

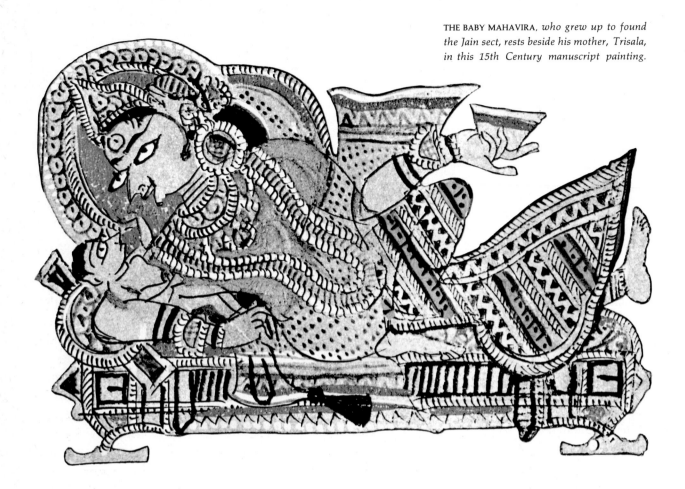

THE BABY MAHAVIRA, *who grew up to found the Jain sect, rests beside his mother, Trisala, in this 15th Century manuscript painting.*

but actions sullied its purity. By rigorous abstention from evil behavior, man could shed his impurities just as by action he had gathered them; then, free of its masses of impurities and restored to its pristine state, the soul would cease to be reborn. To a Jain, then, the purpose of life was to cleanse the soul.

Soul-cleansing was a difficult job, since virtually all activity produced impurities. The only way to achieve salvation was to enter a monastery and try, in effect, to do nothing at all. Mahavira warned against such actions as stealing and lying, which would add to the impurities already covering the soul. Especially did he warn against violence to other souls. Since everything in the universe had a living soul, killing any form of life would produce terrible spiritual results. So seriously did Mahavira and his monks take the ban on killing that they carried whisks to brush aside insects they might otherwise step on, and wore masks over their noses and mouths lest they accidentally breathe in any living creature. All beings, Mahavira said, "shun destruction and cling to life. They long to live. To all things life is dear."

Today, orthodox Jains consume no meat and eat only in the daytime to prevent accidental harm to insects in the dark.

Contrasting with this veneration of life, however, was a paradoxical delight in death. For a Jain the supreme accomplishment was to commit suicide by starvation. This was the end Mahavira chose for himself. He fasted to death at the age of 72, leaving a sect that survives to this day.

Mahavira's regimen was harsh, but his teachings caught on and endured. The ascetic life that he extolled as a means to salvation was a well-established Indian tradition. But he had taken old ideas and given them new life. By defining karma so graphically, he made concrete and understandable a process that the brahmans had presented as an abstraction. Although he asserted that only as a monk could a man achieve salvation, he and his followers always welcomed laymen to retreats in Jainist monasteries and encouraged them to emulate the lives of monks as closely as possible. They could indeed live as good Jains in the world outside the monasteries, for Mahavira's precepts of honesty and fairness were compatible with the rising urban life. Jains could not be farmers, because plowing destroyed creatures that lived in the soil, but with easy conscience they could be merchants in an India that was increasingly busy with commerce and trade. They soon slipped comfortably into the social framework as a separate but fully accepted religious group.

Jainism answered certain needs and appealed to certain elements of Indian society, and thus it had a hardier life than most of the sects that preceded it. But a more charismatic figure and a religion of greater import were to come from another person. That person was Siddhartha Gautama, better known as the Buddha—one of the two or three most inspired and inspiring figures in the history of mankind.

All great heroes are surrounded by legends that obscure the facts of their lives, and the Buddha is no exception. Under the legends lie a few historical facts known to be true. Siddhartha Gautama, like Mahavira, was the son of a lord of a tribe that lived in the foothills of the Himalayan Mountains. He was born sometime in the Sixth Century B.C., probably in 567. From that point the legends take over. According to one tale, he was conceived when his mother was visited in a dream by a sacred white elephant, which touched her left side with a white lotus held in its trunk. Gautama's birth is described in equally miraculous terms: he came from his mother's right side while she stood in a garden. Light flooded the world, the blind saw, the deaf heard and the halt and maimed ran toward the infant. The babe took seven steps in each of the four directions, then announced: "This is my last birth—henceforth there is no more birth for me." In his tiny footprints, lotus blooms burst forth.

As the son of a rich nobleman, he lived in royal manner. He had the run of three palaces, the entertainment of 40,000 dancing girls and a herd of elephants decked in silver ornaments. He is said to have been handsome, a fine student and a skilled athlete. At 16 he married a highborn lady, whom he won by feats of prowess at a contest. But while still in his twenties, he was apparently stirred by a sort of divine discontent.

No factual history tells how Gautama came to assume a religious calling, but the legend of the Four Signs grew up to explain his undertaking. Five days after his miraculous birth, the legend says, soothsayers predicted that the boy would be a Universal Emperor unless he were summoned to become a Universal Teacher by four signs, which would reveal to him the misery of the world. These alternatives permitted only one choice to Gautama's father, a worldly and aristocratic man, who determined that the prince should see no human sorrow and ordered the royal parks cleared of the sick and destitute. But the gods arranged that one day, while riding through the grounds, Gautama should come upon a bent and decrepit old man. He asked his charioteer what this creature was, and from the answer learned that all men age. The First Sign of the prophecy had been fulfilled. Not long afterward, on another ride through the park, Gautama saw a man disfigured with sores and trembling with ague; from this encounter, the Second Sign, he learned that men suffer sickness. The Third Sign was a dead man; this taught him the fact of death. The Fourth Sign was a beggar unmistakably contented although he wore nothing but a yellow garment and carried a bowl for begging food. From this last sign, Gautama learned that men could find peace in withdrawing from the world, and he understood that this was to be his own destiny.

Not long afterward he slipped away from home in the middle of the night, bidding only a silent farewell to his sleeping family because he feared he would not be able to leave his wife and newborn child if they were awake and smiling at him. Attended by his charioteer and a host of demigods—who silenced the clatter of his horse's hooves so he could get away undetected—he galloped away from the palace. Nearing a forest, he took off his princely robes and donned some beggarly rags handed him by one of the demigods. Then he sent his charioteer back to the palace with locks of his hair as trinkets for his family. His horse dropped dead of grief.

Gautama began his attempt to discover "the realm of life in which there is neither age nor death" when he was 29. He approached the task in the traditional way—by going to sit at the feet of a guru, a learned teacher who taught the wisdom of the Upanishads. But the teachings failed to satisfy him, and he left the guru to try another traditional way of finding salvation, the life of austerity. Joining a band of five ascetics, he retreated to a forest, where he outdid his companions in the rigors he imposed on himself. He ate only a single bean a day and eventually grew so thin that he said he could touch his spine when he put his hand on his stomach. After six years of this regimen he collapsed one day and revived only when a village maiden happened along and gave him some gruel to eat. When he recovered sufficiently for reflection, the idea came to him that without the use of his body he could hardly use his head to gain enlightenment; severe self-denial was not the path to knowledge that he was seeking. His fellow-ascetics gave him up as a reprobate, and Gautama turned to solitary meditation.

This time, determined to succeed, he settled himself under a fig tree outside the town of Gaya, near Banaras, and resolved not to rise until he understood the mystery of life. Like Jesus, he was assailed by a demon with all manner of temptations, but he withstood the taunts until the demon fled in defeat. After Gautama had sat beneath the tree for 49 days, he awakened from a trance to see the condition of mankind with superhuman clarity. Thus he became the Buddha, the "Enlightened One." For another 49 days he remained under the tree, pondering the riddles he had solved, then set out for the holy city of Banaras to teach what he had learned. In a park outside that city he delivered his first sermon. His only audience was the band of five ascetics who had abandoned him before; they turned to him now as rapt disciples. The sermon was to become one of the most celebrated in the history of religion.

In this sermon the Buddha proclaimed the Four Noble Truths and the Eightfold Path, concepts that have remained fundamental to Buddhism, though many have changed greatly.

The First Noble Truth is that life is *dukkha*, a word usually translated as suffering. But in the Pali language, in which the Buddhist scriptures were first recorded, the word is applied to an axle that separates from its wheel or a bone that comes loose from its socket. In the Buddha's statement, life is out of kilter; that is why man is doomed to suffer.

The Second Noble Truth is that the reason for suffering is *tanha*—a word that is usually translated as thirst or desire, but in the Buddha's terms meant specifically a craving for individual fulfillment. So long as man strives for himself he will remain dislocated from the universe at large, and he will suffer. In this the Buddha was building on an idea from the Upanishads—that every man should seek identification with all other things. The Buddha, however, did not regard this

A BENIGN FACE OF THE BUDDHA *is shown in a Second Century B.C. sculpture from Gandhara. The dot between the eyebrows and the protuberance on top of the head are traditional identifying marks intended to symbolize the Buddha's great spiritual powers.*

identification process as involving a universal spirit like the Brahman of the Upanishads.

The Third Noble Truth is that the craving for individuality must be overcome; and the Fourth Noble Truth is that the means for overcoming it is the Eightfold Path.

The Eightfold Path, like the Ten Commandments, is a code to live by; but unlike the Commandments, which are held to be equally true and binding for all men at all times, the Path is a set of rules to be followed in ascending order; until the first step has been mastered, one cannot expect to succeed in the later steps.

The first step on the Eightfold Path is Right Understanding. Man must know what he is about if he is to win salvation; he must know the Four Noble Truths. The second is Right Purpose: he must aspire to reach salvation. The third is Right Speech: he must not lie and he must not commit slander, for both arise out of the will to perpetuate individuality, and thereby shut the aspirant off from salvation. The fourth is Right Behavior, toward which the Buddha offers five precepts: Do not kill; do not steal; do not lie; do not be unchaste; do not drink intoxicants. The fifth is Right Means of Livelihood: one must be engaged in an occupation conducive to salvation—preferably the monastic life. The sixth is Right Effort: one must exercise will power if he would succeed. The seventh is Right Awareness: one must constantly examine one's behavior and, like a patient in psychoanalysis, trace it to its cause, trying to understand and remove the cause of misdeeds. The eighth and final step on the Path is Right Meditation: one must ponder often and deeply on ultimate truth if one is to find salvation.

Through the legends of the Buddha comes a picture of a world hero who is an extremely endearing and human person. On one occasion he encountered an outcaste who lived by scavenging rubbish heaps in the street. The outcaste, accustomed to the rule that he remove himself from the presence of the upper castes, cowered against the wall of the nearest building. But the Buddha broke convention and spoke to the frightened creature. "Sunita," he said, "what to you is this wretched mode of living? Can you endure to leave the world?" The poor scavenger was overcome. "If such as I may become a monk of yours, may the Exalted One suffer me to come forth." The Buddha took him into his religious order, where he excelled as a monk.

On another occasion a woman approached him carrying the corpse of her only child; she beseeched the Buddha to bring the baby to life. He asked her to bring him some mustard seed from a family in which no one had died. She searched all over, but naturally she could find no family that had never suffered death. Finally understanding the meaning of his request, she gave up the search, then entered the Buddhist order as a nun.

Several aspects of the Buddha's teachings displayed insight of astonishing power for the time. First, he taught in the vernacular instead of the arcane Sanskrit in which the teachings of the Upanishads were preserved, thus making religious ideas available to far more people than before. Second, he opened a path to salvation that was independent of complex ritual—anyone could follow the path, provided he exercised self-effort. Finally—and in this the Buddha stands alone among the religious leaders of the world—he refused to engage in metaphysical speculation about the universe. The result was the unique phenomenon of a religion without a god, without worship, even without a human soul. The Buddha seems never to have reconciled the meaning of karma and transmigration in the absence of a soul, but that did not deter people from flocking to him. In time hundreds of monasteries all over

the land contained thousands of monks and nuns seeking salvation along his Eightfold Path.

He made a stunning impact on the India of his day. The Upanishads had taken account of man's growing moral conscience, but they were esoteric in their beliefs and were made even more inaccessible to most of the people by the fact that they were written in Sanskrit. And insofar as salvation was contingent on knowledge of the truths in the Upanishads, it was denied to the lower castes. The Buddha made it available to all.

If Buddhism was unique, as a religion without a god and without worship, it did not long remain so. During his life some of the Buddha's followers tried to deify him—a move he resisted; later their heirs succeeded. In time the religion split into sects, as all religions are wont to do, and the major divisions came to be called the Greater and Lesser Vehicles (vehicles because both claim to carry man to salvation). The Greater Vehicle, which has the larger number of followers (some 250 million throughout Asia today), not only deified the Buddha, but supplied the metaphysical scheme he had resolutely omitted: a cosmology adorned with heavens and hells and peopled with saints, as well as a worship embellished with incense, candles and holy water.

Oddly enough, although Buddhism spread all over the world, it eventually disappeared from India. Its message was not lost, however. Many of the noblest principles of Buddhism worked their way deep into Indian thought. By the time of the Buddha the religion of the brahman priests was already changing of itself, reflecting the growing moral conscience of the times. Yet to come was the final development of Hinduism—a religion sufficiently broad and flexible to accommodate the ancient gods, the philosophic speculations of the Upanishads, the censure of violence inspired by Jainism and the ethics of Buddhism.

THE BUDDHA'S PATH TO WISDOM

A MASSIVE SHRINE, *the Buddhist memorial at Sanchi is guarded by four ornately carved gates.*

One of the most remarkable—and influential—men who ever lived was born in the foothills of the Himalayas during the Sixth Century B.C. Known to his followers as the Buddha, or "Enlightened One," he was a royal prince who abandoned his position to become a religious teacher and in the course of his ministry created, perhaps inadvertently, an entirely new faith. Within his band of followers, the Buddha ignored the traditional Indian distinctions of caste; his mission was to bring solace to all suffering humans. Buddhism, the faith he founded, passed beyond India's borders into Southeast Asia, Tibet, Mongolia, China, Korea and Japan to become one of the world's great religions and the most popular faith in the Orient. In its native land, however, it almost completely died out, gradually absorbed by the later development of Hinduism. Among the surviving reminders in India of early Buddhism are the stupas, or memorial shrines, that were often built to house the relics of the Buddha or his disciples. The most impressive stupa still standing (*above*) was erected at Sanchi in central India, and decorated by sculptors in the First Century B.C. with beautifully carved scenes from the life of the Enlightened One.

THE BODHI TREE

THE WHEEL OF THE DOCTRINE

A STUPA, OR MEMORIAL SHRINE

THE RENUNCIATION OF A LIFE OF PLEASURE

The first important discovery the Buddha made was that all men were born to suffer. During his childhood, the Buddha—or Gautama, as he was called before his enlightenment—was carefully protected from this realization. As the legends recount, his father, the king of the city of Kapilavastu in Nepal, feared his son might renounce his title and become an ascetic. The father therefore guarded Gautama from all painful sights that might awaken in him religious feelings of compassion. He and his young wife were well housed in sumptuous palaces, and surrounded by luxuries.

Despite these precautions, however, the young man went on occasional drives in the city, and during these drives encountered four men—an old man, a sick man, a dead man and, finally, a monk. Suddenly recognizing the range of human woes, Gautama decided to follow the example of the monk. He stole away from his house in the dead of night and traded his princely clothes for simple robes. Because early Buddhist sculptors probably felt it would be sacrilegious to portray Gautama himself in their carvings, they indicated his presence by such symbols as those shown at left.

SYMBOLS OF THE BUDDHA (left), used instead of human likenesses, include the Bodhi tree, under which the Buddha was enlightened; a wheel, representing his teaching; and a Buddhist shrine.

AN EMPTY CHARIOT, viewed by the people of Gautama's hometown, symbolized the story of his four excursions, during which he saw four men who were to change his whole way of life.

A TRIUMPH OVER WORLDLY TEMPTATIONS

Although Gautama believed that to live was to suffer, he did not discover how to escape from suffering until he attained enlightenment. After he left his family he joined a band of five monks who practiced extreme austerities. But starvation and exposure to the elements failed to produce any deep insights, so he left the band and resumed a normal, though frugal, existence.

One day, however, he sat under a tree (called the Bodhi, or "Wisdom," tree) to meditate, resolving not to rise until he had found ultimate wisdom. An evil god called Mara sought to distract Gautama with demons, fire and visions of sensual delight, but to no avail.

Concentrating deeply, Gautama found the truths he had sought for so long. Like most Indians, he believed that each time a man died he was fated to be reborn into a harsh world. Now he saw that the cause of rebirth was the craving people felt for life's illusory pleasures; if a man could uproot all his desires he would escape rebirth. With this insight, Gautama achieved enlightenment.

PREPARING TO MEDITATE, *Gautama (indicated by the empty seat under the tree) is attended by winged deities—and tempted by Mara's daughter, shown standing to the right of the tree.*

LEERING DEMONS, *seen here in two parts of a carved frieze, were sent by Mara to frighten the meditating Gautama. They tried to infect him with worldly vices, but Gautama proved incorruptible.*

EIGHT STEPS
TO ENLIGHTENMENT

Once he had achieved enlightenment himself, the Buddha wanted to lead other men on the same path. During his first sermon, he addressed the five ascetics with whom he had once practiced mortifications of the flesh. He informed these monks—and an assembly of demigods—that the way to wisdom lay between the two extremes of austerity and self-indulgence.

This path consisted of eight steps. The first two, Right Understanding and Right Purpose, required an individual to have a correct knowledge of Buddhist principles and the will to strive after perfection. Right Speech, Right Behavior and Right Means of Livelihood produced a well-disciplined and moral life. Such virtuous conduct led him toward Right Effort, Right Awareness and Right Meditation.

The sermon so impressed the monks that they were converted on the spot —and the Buddha had begun his long career of bringing solace to multitudes.

ACHIEVING FULL WISDOM *(left), the Buddha —symbolized by a disk on the seat beneath the tree—receives the praise of divinities. While four gods, lords of the four cardinal directions, offer homage on earth, winged deities bestow on him garlands of flowers.*

THE FIRST SERMON, *called "Setting the Wheel of the Doctrine in Motion," was attended by the gods of the four directions and their female companions. The wheel in this carving stands for the Buddha's teachings and also for the presence of the Buddha himself.*

OFFERING HONEY, *a monkey extends a bowl toward the Buddha's throne. After the gift is accepted, the monkey dances (right).*

A MESSAGE GIVEN TO ALL LIVING CREATURES

As the Buddha converted more and more people to his beliefs, he created a community of monks that ignored virtually all distinctions among men. Although he did not challenge the rigid caste structure of ordinary Indian society, within his own band of monks he insisted on complete equality. "No one is an outcaste by birth, nor is anyone a

WALKING ON WATER, *the Buddha—indicated by a calm path among the waves—converts a brahman, seated in the boat (center, above).*

brahman by birth," the Buddha said; "it is by deeds that a person becomes a brahman."

In this democratic spirit, the Buddha imparted his wisdom to all he met. When he came upon a proud brahman who was skeptical about his teachings, the Buddha willingly performed the miracle of walking on water *(above)*, dispelling the brah-

man's doubts and later converting him to the faith. Kings and common laborers alike were accepted into the new order, and women were permitted to become nuns. In one fanciful tale, the Buddha even received the devotion of a monkey *(above, left)*; the animal became so excited after this meeting that it died from a surfeit of happiness.

NIRVANA: THE ULTIMATE RELEASE FROM REBIRTH

When he reached the age of 80, the Buddha considered his mission on earth accomplished. During the 45 years of his ministry he had converted thousands, including his own townsmen *(below)*. Now he prepared for the end of his life and for entering into the state that was the ultimate goal of all his followers—nirvana (literally, "extinction"). Achievement of nirvana, considered a complete release from all desires, meant that the believer would never have to be reborn into the world again.

The Buddha died, tradition has it, when he accepted from a pious layman a piece of pork—which he knew was spoiled but which he was too polite to refuse. He ate it, sickened and lay down in a park to die. As he performed his final meditations, he felt himself becoming free of all passions. Turning to his followers, he told them to remember that the things of the world were unreal and were subject to decay. With his last breath he commanded them: "Work out your own salvation with diligence."

ADDRESSING HIS TOWNSMEN *(left)*, the Buddha is surrounded by the nobles of Kapilavastu. During a visit to the town, the Buddha converted most of the citizens, including his wife and his son, who had been born just before the Buddha's departure.

A TOWERING STUPA, symbolizing the Buddha's death and his attainment of nirvana, receives the reverences of human and divine worshipers. While marching around the stupa, some men fold their hands in respect and others wave banners or proffer flowers.

4

ASHOKA, EMPEROR OF PEACE

Some time about the year 320 B.C., a young Indian warrior-king named Chandragupta Maurya set out to build an empire. His qualifications for the job were uncertain, and his prospects must have seemed dubious. Chandragupta's origins were apparently obscure to begin with, and have been further obscured by centuries of legend. His very name has become a subject of dispute: some legends trace the name "Maurya" to the phrase *mayura poshaka*, the title of a lowly caste of peacock tamers, while others derive it from a warrior clan called the Moriyas.

Even the legends that place Chandragupta in the high-born warrior class are curiously vague about his early years. According to one such legend, his father lost his life in a petty war before the boy's birth, and Chandragupta was brought up in an obscure village under the care of a cowherd and, later, of a hunter.

Against whatever odds of birth or upbringing, Chandragupta Maurya attained his ambitions. During his lifetime, he extended his power from a base in the central Ganges Valley east and west to the farthest limits of the Indo-Gangetic plain. His descendants, the emperors of the Mauryan dynasty, held sway over still vaster areas. At its height, the Mauryan Empire was the first great Indian empire of historic times.

The beginnings of that empire reveal a pattern of political development that has been repeated in different places and at different times throughout world history. On the one hand, there was a strong native state, constantly growing in extent and power—in this case, the kingdom of Magadha on the central Ganges River. On the other, there was a region under foreign domination—the region to the northwest, the Punjab and the Indus Valley, ruled successively by Persians and Greeks. In the course of time the native state, led by Chandragupta, established its supremacy over all of northern India from the Bay of Bengal to the Arabian Sea.

Magadha had certain advantages from the start. As much as 200 years before Chandragupta's time, the kingdom had begun to develop a river trade that brought it into contact with sailors and merchants far up and down the Ganges. The plains surrounding Magadha had fertile soil, forests thick

A RULER'S MEMORIAL, *a column capped by four scowling lions, is one of the monuments erected by the Mauryan emperor Ashoka to proclaim his edicts and policies. Modern India preserves the lion figure on its official seal.*

with timber, rich mines and herds of elephants that could be used for work or for war. Gradually, the wealthy, cosmopolitan state began to expand. Bimbisara, a Magadhan king of the Sixth Century B.C., won a foothold in the lands to the west and north by marriage alliances, then conquered the lands to the southeast that controlled trade in the delta of the Ganges. His successors pushed the frontiers still farther, and made Magadha the strongest of the kingdoms in the Ganges plain. Finally, about 322 B.C., the kingdom reached a turning point when Chandragupta Maurya seized the throne.

It may not have seemed a turning point at the time. The legends of Chandragupta's life, which are so vague in describing his origins, do little to explain his rise to power. But it is clear that he emerged as a skillful military leader who opposed and eventually overthrew the legitimate kings of Magadha. And once in supreme command, he turned his eyes westward, beyond the Ganges plain to the Indus Valley and the country of the far northwest.

These western regions had had a very different history from that of northeast India. In 531 B.C. Cyrus the Great, the founder of the Persian Empire, led an invading army across the Hindu Kush mountains and into India; by 518 one of his successors, Darius I, had conquered the Indus Valley and the Punjab. Through these military victories, northwest India became a province—called the "twentieth satrapy"—of the Persian Empire. For nearly 200 years the Persians ruled the region with an iron hand. According to the Greek historian Herodotus, the twentieth satrapy paid more tribute to Persia than any other division of the empire, and a contingent of Indian troops served under the Persian emperor Xerxes in his invasion of Greece in 479 B.C. On the other hand, the peoples of northern India gained something from the Persian occupation. Sophisticated Persian styles in art and architecture were influential throughout the region; it was an educational center to which came well-born young men from such Indian kingdoms as Magadha; and some historians argue that even the expansionist policies of Magadha were inspired by the Persian example.

It was not the Indians, however, who finally ended Persian rule in the region. In 331 B.C. the Macedonian conqueror Alexander the Great won a crucial victory against Persian forces near the Tigris River. Having destroyed Persian power at its source, Alexander drove eastward, and in 327 entered India to take possession of the Persian territories there. His troops fought their way into the northwest, defeating both Persian and native Indian forces and planting settlements as they came. For a moment in the history of northwest India, it seemed that one foreign ruler would be permanently replaced by another.

But only for a moment. Within two years Alexander had left India, never to return; in 323, with his dream of ruling the world completely shattered, he died in Babylon, far to the west. In a sense, it was the Indian subcontinent itself that defeated the would-be world conqueror. Alexander had come to India with the false notion that the subcontinent was a small peninsula, with its farther shore only a short distance beyond the Indus River. Once he crossed the Indus, however, he realized that unknown immensities lay before him. What was more important, his troops, wearied in battles against local Indian forces and terrified by tales of fierce peoples and frightful beasts in the unknown lands ahead, refused to go farther. And the long retreat to Babylonia, through the searing deserts that border the Arabian Sea, weakened Alexander's army and broke his power. A modern historian, comparing Alexander with Napoleon Bonaparte, another would-be conqueror of vast

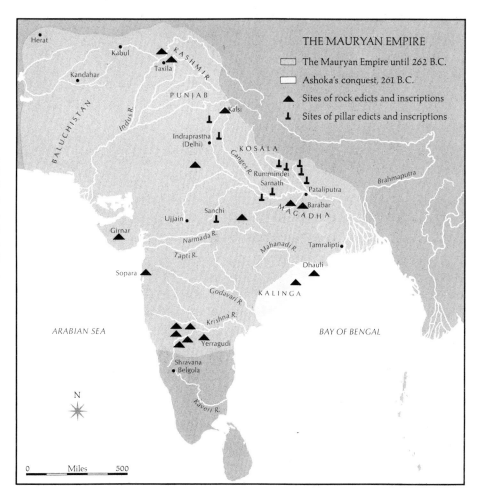

INDIA'S FIRST GREAT EMPIRE, *the Mauryan, was founded by Chandragupta, who seized the throne of the Magadha kingdom in 322 B.C. He and his son annexed all of northern and central India; his grandson, Ashoka, who ruled from 269 to 232 B.C., conquered Kalinga and governed most of the subcontinent, as shown by the far-flung sites of monuments and rocks carved with his edicts.*

but thwarted ambitions, has said that "the Indian expedition was Alexander's Moscow campaign."

From the point of view of northeast India, however, Alexander's departure created a great military and political opportunity. The small outposts and garrisons left behind by the Macedonians soon withered away, and the Indian kings of the northwest, who had held no real power for centuries, were too weak to take command. A power vacuum had been formed—and Chandragupta Maurya was eager to fill it. He assumed the Magadhan throne about two years after Alexander's retreat from India and began almost at once to move in on the northwest.

Within a decade, Chandragupta made himself master of the Punjab and the Indus Valley. In 305 B.C., he met and defeated Seleucus Nicator, a successor of Alexander's who was attempting to recover the dead emperor's Indian provinces. Instead of regaining lost lands, Seleucus had to give up

lands of his own in the mountainous northwest—Baluchistan, and the regions of Kabul, Kandahar and Herat in what is now Afghanistan. (Legends suggest that as part of the arrangement Seleucus also gave his daughter to Chandragupta in marriage, while the Indian ruler made a regal gift of 500 elephants to the man he had defeated.

Chandragupta was now an emperor rather than a king. From his capital at Pataliputra, on the site of the present-day city of Patna in northeast India, he ruled an empire that included the plains of the Indus and Ganges Rivers and the high country of the northwest. To this realm, his descendants added even larger territories. Chandragupta's son Bindusara, who reigned from about 298 to 273 B.C., probably extended the empire's border southward, deep into the Deccan plateau and as far down the western coast as modern Mysore. Ashoka, Chandragupta's grandson and the third king of the Mauryan dynasty, brought the Mauryan Empire to its height. During his long reign from 269 to 232 B.C., he conquered Kalinga, a region on the eastern coast of India.

The relative precision with which these events can be dated reflects a significant development in Indian history. For the first time, genuine historical documents can be called upon for a clear picture of political change and—in even greater detail—social conditions. There are, for example, the reports of a Greek diplomat, Megasthenes, who served as Seleucus Nicator's ambassador at the court of Chandragupta for several years. There is a manual of politics and statecraft called the *Arthashastra*, attributed to Chandragupta's chief minister, a brahman named Kautilya. Most important, there are Ashoka's edicts, carved on pillars and rocks, which provide both a record of the time and a statement of its highest ethical code.

To be sure, these sources have their limitations. The diplomat Megasthenes, for instance, wrote in much the fashion that an ambassador might write today; his accounts of Chandragupta's empire are short on information about the life of ordinary people, but full of details about the organization of the state and the life of the court. From these accounts, it is clear that Chandragupta—and, in all likelihood, his descendants—imposed strict, highly centralized rule over the vast Mauryan realm. The emperor himself held final authority over military, legislative and judicial matters. Below him was a rigid centralized bureaucracy, with separate departments for such areas as trade and commerce, agriculture, forestry and public works, all operating independently of each other and directly responsible to the emperor. Officials of these departments made their headquarters in the capital, Pataliputra, but maintained staffs of supervisors and subordinate officials at local centers.

The smallest of these local centers were the villages, each with its own headman. The headman reported to the officials of a district, consisting of a group of villages. The governor or chief official of a district reported in turn to the officials of a province, which consisted of a group of districts. Four of these provinces, with capitals at Taxila, Ujjain, Dhauli and Suvarnargiri, have been identified. Each province was headed by a viceroy, often a member of the royal family, who reported directly to the central government.

In this hierarchy, the district governor often held more power than his intermediate rank would imply. His association with his region often predated the empire, and he seems to have exercised semi-independent control over his land and villages. In addition, many a governor apparently took as part of his job the sly supervision of his viceregal superior. But ambitious governors represented only one of the dangers that Chandragupta had to guard against. His huge empire was a new one, and consisted of a motley collection of petty, pugnacious states. Despite all the checking and double-checking of government agents, conspiracy and rebellion were a constant threat. To meet this threat, the emperor set up an elaborate system of personal precautions and repressive controls.

For fear of assassination, Chandragupta was constantly guarded and frequently changed his sleeping quarters. When a rebel or traitor was detected, the death penalty followed as a matter of course; to obtain confessions or inflict punishment, frightful tortures were devised. In the *Arthashastra*, an 18-day cycle of tortures is described, with a different method of torture suggested for each day. To justify such procedures, the manual provided one of the most cold-blooded aphorisms in political history: "Government is the science of punishment."

A despotism as ruthless as this needed ruthless organizations to support it—and such organizations came into being. Chandragupta created repressive extensions of his personal authority, in his spy system and his army, which ranged the empire with no check on their power and no formal attachments at the local level.

The spy system was a gigantic secret service that both funneled information to the emperor and carried out his secret orders. "The ablest and most trustworthy men are appointed to fill these offices," reported Megasthenes. The *Arthashastra*, which devotes two chapters to the system, gives a fuller picture. From that highly realistic work, one modern student, A. L. Basham, has drawn up a list of different kinds of spies: "Brahmans unable to make a living by their learning, merchants fallen on evil days, barbers, astrologers, humble servitors, prostitutes, peasants." One group of secret agents consisted of orphans raised from childhood to pass themselves off as fortune tellers or holy men, because such men were especially trusted by the populace. Another group was "that of the desperado, recruited from professional prize-fighters; the main duty of such an agent was the assassination of those enemies of the king for whom a public trial was not expedient."

The army, of course, needed no such secrecy to carry on its work. Its original task was to conquer new territory and to pacify the outposts of empire. The *Arthashastra*, typically free of any trace of morality or altruism, described this function in words that might have been written by an Indian Machiavelli: "With increasing strength, make war; when you have a clear advantage over a neighbor, march against him; do not disturb the customs of a newly conquered people." But Chandragupta's army had a domestic function, too: its garrisons throughout the empire held the people in check and suppressed the smallest sign of sedition or revolt.

To perform both these functions, the imperial army was magnificently equipped. At its height, it numbered 700,000 men, with 9,000 elephants and 10,000 chariots. According to Megasthenes, its op-

erations were supervised by a central War Council of 30 officials, who held responsibility for everything from food and transport to the maintenance of the proper servants to beat drums, carry gongs and perform a host of military ceremonies. In fact, the troops seem to have had a wonderfully easy time of it when they were not on the field. Megasthenes reported that Indian soldiers "lead a life of supreme freedom and enjoyment. They have only military duties to perform. Others . . . attend on them in the camp . . . take care of their horses, clean their arms, drive their elephants, prepare their chariots and act as their charioteers."

Protected by this pampered army and by his hidden army of spies, Chandragupta led a public life of enormous pomp and splendor. The occasions on which he appeared outside his palace walls were generally celebrated by gorgeous royal processions. The emperor, wearing fine muslin robes embroidered in purple and gold, was borne forth on a gold litter lavishly decorated with pearls. His guards rode elephants emblazoned with gold and silver; some of these guards carried trees on which live birds perched, and a flock of trained parrots hovered over the emperor or whirled about his head.

Such processions were often part of one or another religious festival, but the emperor also indulged himself in sports, particularly hunting. His guards and fellow participants in the hunt were comely women, armed with swords and riding as swiftly and freely as men. The spectator sport that most delighted him, as it did so many kings and emperors after him, was racing, though he also enjoyed watching fights between wild bulls, rams, rhinoceroses and elephants. Chandragupta's favorite racers were a breed of trotter oxen which could run as fast as horses.

But there was another side of the emperor's life, and a far more important one. Despite all the cruelty of his rule and the vanity of his public displays,

A NATURE-GODDESS, *standing beneath lotus flowers, was carved as a guardian figure for a Buddhist monument. Such sculpture was inspired by the patronage of the Mauryan emperor Ashoka.*

Chandragupta devoted himself to public business and the public good. The *Arthashastra*, generally so heartless in its advice, contains this wise admonition to the head of state:

In the happiness of his subjects lies a king's happiness,
In the welfare of his subjects, his welfare.
A king's good is not that which pleases him,
But that which pleases his subjects.

It is clear that, according to his own lights, Chandragupta worked unstintingly for his subjects' happiness and welfare. Megasthenes reported that "even when the king has his hair combed and dressed, he has no respite from public business." And the emperor did benefit his people. Under his leadership, the empire enjoyed a time of general prosperity and busy trade. Irrigation systems were built and regulated; a network of roads was maintained. To Indians of later times, the reign of Chandragupta Maurya came to represent the beginning of a golden age.

Even the emperor's personal life seems to have undergone a radical change in his last years. According to one tradition, the once-mighty hunter and warrior embraced Jainism, the creed that opposed all violence and killing, even the killing of living things for food. It is said that after 24 years of absolute rule the old empire-builder abdicated his throne to become a Jain monk. He entered the temple of Shravana Belgola—still an active Jain monastery in Mysore—and, in imitation of the founder of the sect, fasted to death.

If Chandragupta represented the promise of a golden age, his grandson, the Emperor Ashoka, brought that promise to fulfillment. During Ashoka's reign, the Mauryan Empire continued to grow and to prosper—but with a difference. For the first time in Indian history, a great state was led by a man who preached goodness, gentleness and non-violence, and who based his own policies on a high ethical code. By his example and his actions, the emperor proved himself, in the words of historian A. L. Basham, "the greatest and noblest ruler India has known, and indeed one of the great kings of the world."

The best testimony to this nobility and greatness exists in Ashoka's own words, inscribed in his famous edicts. Still to be seen on rocks, in caves and on specially erected pillars, these inscriptions speak as directly to posterity as they did to the emperor's subjects. About 30 have been discovered, in sites ranging almost 1,500 miles from the Hindu Kush mountains to Mysore, and as far eastward as the coast of the Bay of Bengal. Taken together, the edicts constitute an extraordinary revelation of the thoughts and decisions of a truly great man.

But the edicts are the fruits of Ashoka's maturity. In his early years he seems to have led the conventional military and political apprenticeship of a potential heir to the throne. He probably served as his father's deputy on the field in campaigns of conquest; to gain experience in government, he also served as viceroy in the provinces of Ujjain and Taxila. What is more, his accession to the throne, according to some legends, was violent: and the great military achievement of his reign, the conquest of the region called Kalinga, on India's east coast, was bloody and merciless.

The Kalinga campaign of 261 B.C. proved to be a turning point in Ashoka's life. It was the last war he ever fought and, in one of the best known of his edicts, he told of his revulsion and remorse:

> The Kalingas were conquered by His Sacred and Gracious Majesty when he had been consecrated eight years. 150,000 persons were thence carried away captive, 100,000 were slain and many times that number died. Just after the taking of Kalinga His Sacred Majesty began to follow Righteousness, to love Righteousness, to give instruction in Righteousness. When an unconquered country is conquered, people are killed, they die, or are made captive. Thus arose His Sacred Majesty's remorse for having conquered the Kalingas. . . . Today, if a hundredth or a thousandth part of those who suffered in Kalinga were to be killed, to die or be taken captive, it would be very grievous to His Sacred Majesty. If anyone does him wrong it will be forgiven so far as it can be forgiven.

The "Righteousness" of which Ashoka spoke was almost certainly a reference to the teachings of the Buddha. Though the edicts rarely mention Buddhism, but use instead the more comprehensive phrase "the law of Righteousness," it is clear that the emperor was converted to Buddhism at about the time of the fall of Kalinga. How far he understood or sympathized with the intricacies of Buddhist theology, we cannot tell; some historians have suggested that the emperor deliberately used the ideas of Buddhism as a unifying creed to which all his dissimilar subjects could subscribe. Of his own devotion to Buddhist ideals, however, there can be no doubt. And he was in a position to give the religion powerful support.

During Ashoka's reign a council of theologians met at Pataliputra to codify the Buddhist canon— the laws and principles of a new formal religion. What was more important, the emperor made Buddhism a missionary faith, comparable to such later world religions as Christianity and Islam. According to his own records, he sent emissaries to the kings of Egypt, Macedonia and the Near East, hoping in vain to convert them to his beliefs. Nearer home, he was more successful: Buddhism spread throughout India, though it never became the dominant religion, and Ashoka's son (or, according to some traditions, his brother) converted the king of Ceylon. From there Buddhism spread to the lands of Southeast Asia, where it was to remain strong to the present time.

It was in his own realm, however, that Ashoka was best able to put the humane, benevolent ideals of Buddhism into practice—and his determination to do so took very practical forms indeed. For example, the emperor appointed special "Officers of Righteousness," who went to all parts of the empire to oversee local officials. The officers made certain that local authorities promoted "welfare and happiness . . . among servants and masters, brahmans and rich, the needy and the aged." More specifically, they were responsible for preventing all "wrongful imprisonment or chastisement," and for ensuring special consideration for "cases where a man has a large family, has been smitten by calamity, or is advanced in years."

The amenities of daily life became the emperor's concern. He ordered medicinal herbs planted for the use of all his subjects, and took thought for the comfort of his people. In the words of one edict: "I have had banyan trees planted to give shade to man and beast; groves of mango trees I have had planted. . . . I have caused wells to be dug; rest-houses have been erected; and numerous watering places have been provided by me here and there for the enjoyment of man and beast."

In subtler ways, Ashoka tried to teach the doctrine of *ahimsa*, or nonviolence, and the sacredness of all living things. He himself gave up his grandfather's favorite pastime, the hunt, and forbade the killing of animals "which are neither used nor eaten." A curious proclamation on the palace menu shows how far the emperor carried the doctrine in his own life: "Formerly, in the kitchen of his Sacred and Gracious Majesty, many hundreds of thousands of living creatures were slaughtered every day to make curries. But now . . . only three living creatures are slaughtered for curry, to wit, two peacocks and an antelope—the antelope, however, not invariably."

On the level of daily life, the doctrine of *ahimsa* furthered the spread of vegetarianism in India. In more general terms, this doctrine of gentleness and compassion may have affected the fortunes of the Mauryan Empire as a whole. Ashoka renounced war as an instrument of policy and taught his own soldiers that the golden rule, the precept that a man should behave toward others as he would wish them to behave toward himself, was the basic law of life. Ironically, this very idea may also have helped to destroy the great empire that Ashoka ruled so wisely and so well.

Less than 50 years after the emperor's death in 232 B.C., the Mauryan Empire fell to pieces. Ashoka's descendants quarreled over the succession; provincial governors revolted and gained independence for their regions. The Mauryan army lost its vigor and combativeness, and was no longer able to defend the empire against invasion or to control the native populations. Buddhist ideals no longer inspired government policy, and the priestly brahman class, once more advisers to kings, reasserted the old intolerance, the old belief in the separation of peoples.

For centuries afterward, Ashoka himself was almost forgotten, a subject of legend and reminiscence. Over a thousand years later, when scholars began to sift the truth behind the legends, his significance in Indian history was sometimes misunderstood. One 19th Century historian, summarizing Buddhist legends of the emperor's career, remarked that in these legends Ashoka seemed "half monster and half idiot."

Gradually, however, a new insight into the meaning of Ashoka's life and teachings came to prevail. In the 20th Century a great leader of modern India, Jawaharlal Nehru, repeatedly paid tribute to his ancient predecessor. In a letter written to his daughter while he himself was a political prisoner, Nehru set down these words:

> The palace of massive stone is gone, leaving no trace behind, but the memory of Ashoka lives over the whole continent of Asia, and his edicts still speak to us in a language we can understand and appreciate. And we can still learn much from them.

And he ended the letter with a quotation from one of Ashoka's noblest utterances:

> All sects deserve reverence for one reason or another. By thus acting a man exalts his own sect and at the same time does service to the sects of other people.

A FLAMBOYANT LIFE AT COURT

The unbelievable tales of opulence that occasional travelers brought from India were, in fact, the truth. From the time of the Mauryas, who created India's first great empire, the wealth and power of the country were extravagantly displayed in the splendor of court life. At the height of Mauryan glory, in the Third Century B.C., the emperors lived in luxurious palaces decorated with ebony and teak, where they surrounded themselves with hundreds of servants, courtiers and bejeweled dancers, like the girl shown here. Even after the power of the Mauryan potentates declined, the memory of their lavish ways persisted in the imagination of the Indian people. In the centuries that followed, other regimes set up close imitations of Mauryan ceremonies, costumes and architecture. Religion also took on some of this secular magnificence, and gods and holy men were often portrayed as pontifical kings and princes by Indian artists. It is religious pictures—murals adorning a complex of Buddhist shrines in the Ajanta caves in Hyderabad—that provide the most colorful record of the people, activities and luxuries of Indian court life. The paintings were intended to illustrate Buddhist legends, but most of them were made during a prosperous era (400-700 A.D.) when Indians consciously emulated Mauryan ways, and they recapture the regal splendor of that early age.

MAJESTIC POMP OF A ROYAL MARCH

One of the legends illustrated in the Ajanta caves is the tale of a prince who was so richly endowed with the Buddhist virtue of generosity that he gave away most of the royal treasury to the poor. He is shown at the right embarking on a journey, surrounded by mendicants begging for alms.

Like most Indian royalty, the philanthropic prince travels in style. Arrayed in a tiara and necklace, he emerges from the palace gate *(left)* with his princess. The royal pair sets out through the town in a gilded carriage drawn by four matched horses *(center)*, while a tradesman in the background raises his arms in veneration.

An even greater display of magnificence marked the ceremonial processions that Indian emperors frequently made while touring their realms. They were surrounded by an impressive entourage of noblemen, standard bearers, musicians blowing conch shells and a veritable circus of horses and elephants, decked out like the animals at the left in pearls, plumes and gold pendants.

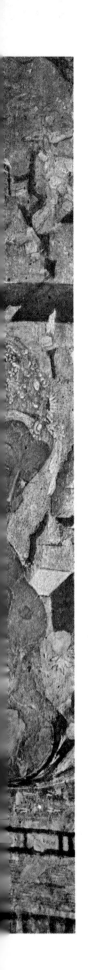

BEDIZENED FIGURES OF ROYALTY

Ostentation was the keynote of life at court. Indian monarchs adorned themselves in a lavish display of finery from the royal storehouses, where gold and silver were sometimes hoarded by the ton, and diamonds and rubies by the pound. The figure at the left, though painted to represent a Buddhist saint, wears the trappings of an earthly prince. A tiara of wrought gold crowns his head. The sapphire in his pearl necklace is a symbol of royalty. He is attended by courtly retainers: a guard brandishing a spear *(far left)*, and his queenly consort seated beside him.

A similar flamboyance marked the king's residence, a complex of pillared halls and lush gardens where peacocks roamed. The maiden at the right sits beneath a gilt portico supported by gold-encrusted pillars. This architectural splendor moved a visitor from China to hyperbole: he wrote that the emperor's palace had been built by spirits, since its elegant carving and inlaid sculpture were worked "in a way which no human hands of this world could accomplish."

RETAINERS: SACRED AND PROFANE

The multitude of courtiers that composed a king's household—in their own way as richly varied as the gems in the royal coffers—are faithfully depicted in the Ajanta murals. Among the most prestigious figures at court were the brahmans, members of a priestly caste who performed rituals, interpreted divine omens and tutored royal children. Many brahmans were devout ascetics, but the particular individual at the left did not live up to the standards of his caste. In the Buddhist legend illustrated, he was entrusted with the care of a king's two grandsons. But instead of giving them an education, he held them for ransom, and he is shown clutching his ill-gotten gold in his arms.

Among the most colorful people at court were the entertainers. Troupes of acrobats, magicians, sword swallowers, snake charmers, wrestlers and actors diverted the king with their performances. Dancers, like the central figure at the right undulating to the rhythms of the musicians around her, made the dance one of India's most expressive art forms.

AMIDST LUXURY,
A DUTY-POINTED TALE

Despite the material splendors that surrounded him, a virtuous ruler was expected to rise above the distractions of court life. From early childhood—an age of three years was the usual starting point—royal heirs were educated in the ideals of hard work, clean living and devotion to the gods. Much of this instruction took the form of morality tales, like the ones illustrated at Ajanta. The parable depicted here warns of the horrifying consequences that could result from giving in to temptation.

This story describes a group of travelers whose ship ran aground on an island off the Indian coast. The island's inhabitants, according to the tale, were a tribe of cannibalistic ogresses who had the power to transform themselves into seductive maidens. In this guise, the ogresses lured the shipwrecked men with amorous entertainments. The travelers, suspecting no evil and willing to take their pleasure where they found it, responded eagerly. One of them is shown dallying with a voluptuous ogress in a silk-draped pavilion (center, foreground), while behind him to the right other ogresses wave enticingly.

But the travelers paid for their pleasure with their lives. At nightfall, the disguised demons reverted to their true form (left)—icy-eyed, frizzle-haired furies who cut the throats of their victims and drank their blood.

Such lurid lessons in the wages of sin were a cornerstone of education at courts that, rich beyond comparison and crowded with temptations to pleasure, governed the large and complex realms of the Mauryan emperors and the monarchs who were to succeed them.

5
GLORY OF THE GUPTAS

Every great people enjoys certain prolonged moments of supreme vigor and delicate organization, when shared attributes combine to create a splendid culture. For Europeans, such a moment occurred in the Renaissance or, going further back, in the "Glory that was Greece" and the "Grandeur that was Rome." For the Hindus of India, the greatest of all ages took place between 320 and 467 A.D., when a dynasty of kings called the Guptas ruled the northern part of the subcontinent. During those years peace, prosperity and material well-being prevailed to a degree unmatched in India before or since. Hindu literature, sculpture, painting, architecture and science reached creative peaks. At the time, in the words of one historian, India was "possibly the happiest and most civilized region in the world."

An age like this one, which is golden while it lasts and proves a culture's greatness forever after, is never a sudden or rootless event. In India, it was over 500 years in the making—years of confusion and apparent aimlessness while India, as the historian Percival Spear has put it, "was getting its second breath before the next outburst of creative activity." The first outburst, of course, had been the Mauryan Empire, which united nearly all of India during the Third Century B.C. During the centuries after the Mauryan unity, disunity was the rule, and northern India remained split into pugnacious small kingdoms and independent dynasties. Contributing to the internal disorder were waves of invasions from Persia, Afghanistan and Central Asia, but while the invaders intensified India's chaos, they also made important contributions to her future development.

The first invaders, in the Second Century B.C., were Greeks from Bactria, in Central Asia north of the Hindu Kush mountains, where the generals of Alexander the Great had founded kingdoms. Then came people known as Shakas or Scythians, from the same Oxus River region, and Parthians, or Pahlavas, who probably migrated from the Iranian plateau. Still later invaders were the Kushans, descendants of Central Asian nomads who had been forced from their native land to Bactria after the building of the Great Wall of China.

Each of these groups came to stay, displacing

AN AURA OF SERENITY *pervades a face of the Buddha carved in northern India about the Fifth Century A.D. During the latter part of the Gupta period, religious sculpture flourished among Buddhists and Hindus alike.*

local authorities and earlier invaders to carve out north Indian kingdoms of greater or lesser importance. The Shakas established themselves in the northwest, where they built up and controlled a lucrative overland trade with Central Asia; the Bactrian Greeks helped to develop a maritime trade between India and Persia and Arabia.

In southern India, the invaders never penetrated. Indeed, southern India remained an area apart through all the centuries of northern turmoil. Mauryan control had never been strong in the south; even during the reign of the great Mauryan emperor Ashoka, the extreme south boasted three completely independent kingdoms—the Cholas, the Pandyas and the Cheras—and these kingdoms remained independent. The people there were a distinct ethnic group, not Aryans but descended from the Dravidians who had lived in this part of the world from prehistoric times; their language, Tamil, was unrelated to northern languages. Southern political, economic and religious traditions were consequently different from the north, and the history of "Tamil Land" tended to be quite separate from that of Aryan India. From the time of the Mauryan Empire to the end of the 14th Century, the south for the most part went its own way.

In the north each of the successive waves of invaders left its mark on India. But only one of the many groups arriving in the centuries between the Mauryan and Gupta Empires was able to establish an extensive and durable kingdom. These people were the Kushans, who, after crossing the Hindu Kush in the First Century A.D., occupied lands in the Punjab, quickly expanded their territories to include most of the northwest, and held sway over the region for almost 200 years. The Kushans are memorable for more than political power, for during their rule and the years immediately following, religion—both Buddhism and Hinduism—underwent significant changes.

A major transformation in Buddhism was taking place during the reign of the greatest of the Kushan kings, Kanishka, who himself became a patron of Buddhism and helped to spread that faith to Central Asia and from there to China and the rest of the Far East. In Kanishka's time, the orientation of Buddhist thought was shifting sharply. The early cult of the teacher Gautama, the Buddha, was becoming the complex religious system called Mahayana Buddhism, which reveres Buddha as a Savior God. The change in Buddhism profoundly affected art. It was during the time of the Kushans that Indian sculptors first carved the figure of the Lord Buddha as supreme God. Hindu sculptors soon began to follow the Buddhist example by depicting the major Hindu deities in symbolic human forms. From this starting point would come the masses of iconographic sculpture that are so much a part of Hinduism.

After the Kushan kingdom broke up, during the Third Century A.D., Buddhism lost the powerful support of the state. Brahmanism had always been the way of life of the majority of the Indian people, and brahmans had always kept control of India's social organization, even after many of the upper classes had become Buddhists (and, in lesser numbers, Jains). Now the brahmans reasserted themselves, building their strength as Buddhism began to decline in India.

The fall of the Kushans is one of the many mysteries of Indian history. Their kingdom may have declined when its home base in Afghanistan fell under Persian control and the source of fresh troops and material abruptly disappeared. If this was the case, the situation in northwestern India during the following hundred years presented a power vacuum curiously like the one that preceded the rise of Chandragupta Maurya back in the Fourth Century B.C. Northern India, disrupted by

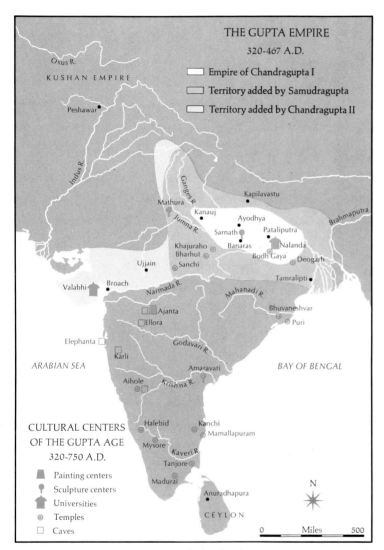

THE GUPTA EMPIRE
320-467 A.D.

Empire of Chandragupta I
Territory added by Samudragupta
Territory added by Chandragupta II

CULTURAL CENTERS
OF THE GUPTA AGE
320-750 A.D.

Painting centers
Sculpture centers
Universities
Temples
Caves

THE APOGEE OF INDIAN CULTURE *was reached under the Gupta emperors. Originally rulers of a small kingdom in the northeast, they expanded their domain until it covered much of northern India. The Guptas lost political power in the Fifth Century A.D., but their cultural influence continued for centuries in places like the University of Nalanda and the painting center of Ajanta.*

petty wars among petty kingdoms, may have been ripe for the taking, much as it had been in the time of Chandragupta Maurya. To make the coincidence complete, the starting place of a new empire was the northeastern kingdom of Magadha—the very place from which Chandragupta Maurya began his rise to power—and the first of the new emperors bore the official name of Chandragupta I.

Whether this founder of the Gupta dynasty was indeed a direct descendant of the Mauryas is questionable, and he certainly followed a different route to power. Unlike his distant predecessor, Chandragupta I began his career with a politic marriage. He himself may have been no more to begin with than an ambitious soldier or a princeling of the Aryan warrior class, but he married a princess of the Licchavi tribe, a strong and influential clan of the northeast. The Licchavis were a martial people, with connections in Nepal and Tibet; they gave the shrewd young king the military power he needed to begin the building of an empire. By the time of his death in 335 A.D., Chandragupta I controlled a large part of northern India, stretching roughly from his starting point in Magadha to modern Allahabad.

His son Samudragupta extended the empire from Assam in the east to the border of the Punjab in the west, and his power was felt far outside the boundaries of his domain. According to an inscribed monument at Allahabad, as far south as the Deccan 12 rulers paid homage to him; in the north, nine kings were "violently uprooted" by him; and in the west, he battled against the Shakas in the region of their capital city, Ujjain.

In the reign of Chandragupta II, Samudra's son, the empire attained its greatest extent. The Shakas were finally defeated, and the emperor held sway completely across northern India, from Bengal to the Arabian Sea, with centers of government at Pataliputra and Ujjain. Once again, however, there was a striking coincidence between the courses of the Mauryan and Gupta Empires. Ashoka, the grandson of the warlike Chandragupta Maurya, had proved to be an apostle of peace. Though Chandragupta II, grandson of the equally ambitious founder of the Gupta Empire, was given the title of Vikramaditya, or "Sun of Prowess," in honor of his military achievements, this greatest of the Gupta emperors was to go down in history as a devoted patron of the arts and the ruler who gave India its greatest era of peace. During his reign centuries of development in sculpture, painting, literature, and science and technology culminated in great achievements that made India the most advanced country of its time.

How Chandragupta nourished this magnificent flowering of culture is one of the mysteries of his reign. Little is known about his methods of government, thanks to the habitual Indian lack of interest in recording historical events. Outsiders were always the best reporters on ancient India, and a Chinese Buddhist monk named Fa-hsien wrote the best extant impressions of Gupta India. Traveling as a pilgrim from one Buddhist monastery to another, Fa-hsien ranged the empire between 401 and 410 A.D., during the reign of Chandragupta II. His main objective was a search for authentic Buddhist texts, and he kept his comments on secular life to a minimum. But his few remarks on social affairs bring home the fact that the Gupta kings gave India an era of calm and plenty in a degree almost unmatched to the present day.

"The inhabitants [of the cities and towns] are rich and prosperous, and vie with each other in the practice of benevolence and righteousness," he wrote. His own pilgrimage was proof that, as he said, a stranger could travel from one end of the country to the other in complete safety and without a passport. Though this was a Hindu empire, the Chinese Buddhist monk never encountered any hostility against himself as a foreigner and a heretic, or any interference with his single-minded Buddhist investigations.

Fa-hsien was moving through India in the atmosphere of a new Hinduism that itself was stimulating the arts. Brahmanism had been expanded to include the devotional cults of Shiva and Vishnu. (The Guptas themselves were patrons of the cult of Vishnu.) Devotion to a chosen deity was usually expressed in homage to an image of the god. Such images were bathed and dressed, offered food and water, adorned with flowers and light, and amused with music and dancing in their homes, the temples. It was these practices that were most influential in the flowering of the arts. Sculptors were needed to create the images, architects to prepare temple homes for the idols.

Sculpture, or more specifically the art of representing the gods in stone, bronze and clay, was the central art. It was also the art that had gone through the longest period of growth from very ancient beginnings.

Indian sculptors had carved tiny figures and exquisite animal seals in prehistoric times. In the Third Century B.C. they had created the realistic, beautifully executed bull and lion capitals on the pillars of Ashoka. Later, sacred Buddhist sites began to acquire carved decorations designed to celebrate the great teacher.

The Buddhist memorials, called "stupas," were originally earthen burial mounds. When a stupa was built over Buddhist relics, the stupa itself became a symbolic object of veneration. And though the mounds themselves were usually bare, the railings and gateways surrounding them became ornate to an extreme. Indians seem always to have felt that, in the words of one art historian, "only things covered with ornaments are beautiful," and "to present an offering without profuse decoration would be an insult to the divinity."

The earliest ornamental figures carved for the stupas included guardian *yakshas*, non-Aryan tree-gods that Buddhists willingly accepted as objects of worship. The *yakshas*, solid, strong, short-necked and thick-bellied, clearly resembled male figurines the Harappans had executed in stone.

Confidence and technique had advanced perceptibly by the First Century B.C. At Bodh Gaya, for example, where the Buddha walked immediately after his enlightenment, the railing around the holy path spills marvelous figures. The Buddha himself is not yet portrayed as a human figure. He is indicated by symbols—a wheel, an empty throne, footprints, the pipal tree. But the old Vedic gods do appear, often symbolizing the Buddha, who had taken their powers to himself. The Vedic sun-god, Surya, for example, represents the Buddha as the sun that illuminates the universe. Other gods play attendant roles. Thus, the Aryan warrior-god, Indra, is shown bearing grass for Gautama, not yet the Buddha, to sit on under the tree where he will become enlightened, while other gods pay homage to the enlightened Buddha.

At Sanchi, the greatest of the early Buddhist stupas, the carvings on gateways show how Buddhism and Hinduism were beginning to meet about the First Century B.C. Alive with their own times, they contain a bewildering variety of images, which are indicated in a summary by A. L. Basham: "Cities are besieged, riders on elephants and horses pass in procession, men and women worship sacred shrines, elephants roam the jungle; lions, peacocks . . . mythical animals and ornate floral designs fill the whole."

This same vigor and bustle of life was carried over from Buddhist carvings to Hindu portrayals of their deities. All Hindu art was religious, but it was secular, too, for Hinduism maintains that everything in the universe is One. Hindu artists were at one with their philosophical tradition; they looked straight at the world they lived in and delighted in what they saw and felt. When a sculptor created an image of a goddess, she embodied his own observation of natural things, for he was celebrating his knowledge that nature was truly one with the gods of the universe. In this way, Indian sculptors infused their work with a combination of spirituality and earthy zest that occasionally confounds the Western world.

By Gupta times, artists had so mastered their technique that they could suggest the zest in a work whose outstanding quality was majestic serenity. The great Gupta sculpture was neither Buddhist nor Hindu. It was Indian. Gupta masterpieces include Buddhas so superbly simplified that they almost seem abstract, and Hindu gods of such realistic detail that they seem almost to breathe—but for both, the tradition was Indian.

Visual arts such as sculpture represent only a part of the artistic heritage of Gupta times. In literature, particularly, the age was one of enormous accomplishment in the classic Sanskrit language. Gupta literature includes, and excels in, such forms as the fable, lyric poetry and the drama.

The fables and fairy tales had great currency and widespread distribution. No other Indian writings have traveled so far or been so influential outside India's borders. The collection of fables called the *Panchantantra*—stories in which animals act and speak like human beings—was read in Baghdad, Byzantium and Cairo, and later, in Europe. Such stories as that of Sinbad the Sailor, in *A Thousand and One Nights*, have an Indian source. And other Indian fables have given themes and plots to generations of Western writers, including Chaucer, Boccaccio and La Fontaine.

In contrast to such writings, courtly poetry did not travel well at all. Its complex techniques

resist translation, and its deeply Hindu spirit baffles or eludes most Westerners.

The courtly tradition in poetry created masterpieces of Sanskrit verse—and also a certain amount of wordplay and poetic fun. One poet composed verses without any sibilants, or "s" sounds, possibly for the amusement of a young prince with a speech defect. Another wrote a poem that meant one thing read left to right, something entirely different when read right to left. Poetry was so much a part of court life that poetic tournaments and competitions were held. High dignitaries—sometimes the king himself—would issue an open challenge to poets to pit their talent and virtuosity against each other. The dignitary tossed out a theme. The competitors twisted it into riddles, phrases with double meaning, puns, verses in a prearranged rhyme scheme, long speeches and erudite short poems. To become a winner of such contests was so important that many competitors were not above slipping a bribe to a judge beforehand to ensure success.

Though far less artificial than poetry in its technique and approach, drama under the Guptas was also for the most part a courtly, secular genre. In this guise it was a relatively new phenomenon, for Indian drama almost certainly began in religious plays performed for the entire community. The earliest Vedic literature contains hymns in dialogue that imply a primitive form of theater. A "frog hymn" in the Rig Veda presupposes men costumed as frogs dancing and singing for the rain-god; the "gambler's hymn" from the Rig Veda suggests men imitating the leaping and falling of dice.

Many centuries elapsed before this simple and direct acting-out of religious ideas was transformed into secular drama, designed specifically for educated audiences and appealing to few outside the noble and cultured classes. By the First Century B.C. it had come to be based upon a complex and rigid set of rules and principles. The guidelines for dramaturgy and theatrical production were established by the literary theorist Bharata in his *Natyashastra,* or "Art of the Play." According to Bharata, drama was designed to stimulate in its audience a dispassionate delight in the contemplation of life as a whole. The dramatist's basic device for arousing this sense of delight was the *rasa*, an isolated emotion or sentiment.

There were eight so-called "stable" *rasas:* love, laughter, anger, sadness, pride, fear, loathing and wonder. In a play, a highly conventional pattern of dialogue or plot, immediately recognizable to the sophisticated audience of the time, evoked the *rasa* of a scene. And by leading such an audience from the erotic *rasa*, to the sad *rasa*, to the fear *rasa*, to the laughter *rasa*, and so on, a playwright produced a complex pattern of *rasas*—in effect, a ninth *rasa*, consisting of the lofty emotion of all emotions combined in one.

This intricate patterning of emotion in scene and dialogue according to the eight basic *rasas* by no means exhausted the playwright's arsenal of conventional devices. Along with the eight "stable" *rasas*, there were no fewer than 33 "unstable" ones. They were subtle refinements or sidelights of the basic eight and ranged from discouragement, weakness and apprehension to joy, dreaming and assurance. Any or all these 33 might make a brief appearance in the course of a play, then be retired to the background.

For all their artificiality, the conventions of Indian courtly playwriting helped to produce a great dramatic literature—but a dramatic literature very different from that of the West. There were, for example, no tragedies or tragic heroes in Indian drama, because no such thing as gratuitous misfortune exists in Hindu thought. Audiences did not leave a Gupta play feeling drained or purged. They left—or were supposed to leave—with a sense of religious peace or serenity. Thus, even the secular plays of the Gupta period summed up the Hindu set of values.

A typical example is the masterwork of India's greatest dramatist and poet, Kalidasa. Probably written during the reign of Chandragupta II, this play deeply impressed and influenced Johann von Goethe, among other Western writers. It tells the story of King Dushyanta and his queen, Shakuntala. Bewitched by his enemies, the king forgets his bride, and the tale plunges into a series of bewildering plot complications. Eventually, a magical ring that Dushyanta had given Shakuntala is discovered by a fisherman in the body of a fish and brought to the king; Dushyanta recovers his memory, and the loving pair is finally reunited. The fairy-tale atmosphere and fabulous incidents, the blissfully happy ending—these might have seemed unsuitable for any serious play by a Western dramatist, but they are exactly right in terms of Kalidasa's intentions and dramatic conventions. *Shakuntala* is a masterpiece of world literature for its rich invention and eloquence. But equally significant to its original audiences was the fact that Kalidasa found the germ of his story in a religious epic, the *Mahabharata*.

The creativity that stirred the Gupta air was not confined to literature and the fine arts. Everything seemed affected by it. Achievements in drama, poetry and plastic arts were equalled by those in science and technology.

The Gupta north was sprinkled with fine universities. The university at Nalanda, for example, attracted students from all over Asia and boasted eight colleges and three libraries. In such institutions, Indian astronomers and mathematicians made advances unmatched anywhere in the world of that time. The astronomers knew that the earth was round and rotated on its axis. The mathematicians, particularly the algebraists, were even more extraordinary. They worked with such sophisticated tools as negative quantities, quadratic equations and the square root of two, and they developed two concepts that were to revolutionize the use of numbers throughout the world. One was the idea and the symbol for zero; the other was the system of so-called Arabic numerals, which was imported from India to the West by Arabian mathematicians centuries later.

On a still more practical level, Indian industry produced tempered steel and iron and a number of fine dyes. Indian textiles were perfected and exported. Cotton, calico, chintz and cashmere are fabrics whose names derive from India, their place of origin, and whose techniques of manufacture were to be borrowed from India by the Arabs and, later, Europeans.

The Gupta dynasty was eventually overthrown by onslaughts by the "White Huns." These invaders from Central Asia were probably not the same Huns who devastated Europe, but they were related to them and achieved the same effect. They began their fierce marauding during the reign of Kumaragupta, the son of Chandragupta II, and by the Sixth Century they had destroyed all Gupta authority along with a number of Gupta palaces, temples, paintings and sculpture. During the years that followed, only one large state existed in northern India, and it was short lived. In 606, a ruler named Harsha began to take over most of the lands the Guptas had held. For the 41 years of his reign, Harsha was another of those unique Indian leaders wise in statesmanship and rich in spirituality. Like the Mauryan emperor Ashoka, Harsha came under the influence of Buddhism and was tolerant of all religions; like the Gupta emperor Chandragupta II, he was a peaceful patron of poetry and art.

After Harsha's death in 647 a new age of northern Indian disunity set in—a period in which, as one historian has put it, "one can but dimly perceive jostling dynasties and commingling peoples." Once again, waves of invaders made their way into India through the mountain passes of the northwest, and the Indo-Gangetic plain was torn by wars among tiny kingdoms and principalities.

One group of military-minded aristocrats, the Rajputs, dominated the course of the next four centuries of Indian history. The clans who came to be called Rajputs may have been descended from the White Huns or from other invaders of the Hunnic period, but they were not themselves a single race or tribe; the very term "rajput," given them after their arrival in India, means simply the sons or relatives of a king. Like many invaders before them, they were accepted by Hindu society as members of the Hindu warrior class, and they considered themselves the rightful rulers of all Indians except brahmans. In their determination to exert their domination, they fought bitterly among themselves, one clan warring on another. But as part of this life of violence they developed and hewed to a code of chivalry that made Rajputs different from all other men.

The Rajput code curiously resembles that of the knights and other nobility of medieval Europe. It emphasized respect for women, succor for the helpless, mercy for a defeated enemy, and the conduct of warfare by forms and military ceremonies of the utmost elegance. Elegance was the keynote, too, of the Rajputs' courtly life. Court poets celebrated Rajput heroism; courtly manners, endlessly refined and elaborated, became a kind of art form of their own.

To be sure, the Rajput code of courtesy, courage and honor did little to bring unity to any Indians, least of all to the Rajputs themselves. But the Rajputs did maintain a sort of cultural continuity that long survived the peak of the Gupta age. Temples were built, statues were carved, plays were written and performed; the arts and sciences so magnificently created under the peaceful Gupta kings were enriched during the centuries of warfare and near chaos. Not until the 13th Century, when Muslim rulers built a new empire in India, would this continuity be seriously threatened.

A UNIVERSE CARVED IN STONE

Like the religions that inspired them, India's temples humble the observer with their grandeur and baffle him with their varied complexity. Some of the oldest are shadowy caverns cut into rocky cliffs by Buddhist monks. Others, erected later by various Hindu sects, are extravagant, many-chambered structures topped by cathedral-like spires. In still other parts of India, temples grew into sprawling walled cities that doubled as artistic and commercial centers, where sages gave classes in the Hindu scriptures and merchants erected bazaars to sell their wares.

The temples were not only complex in layout, but were covered with ornamental carving, often in such abundance that it obscured the basic structure. Each of these carvings had its own symbolic meaning, derived from one of the many different sources of India's cultural tradition. Buddhist lotus flowers, Hindu gods and representations of spirits from India's earliest folk myths were often crowded together in a single sculpted panel, together with figures of elephants, monsters, princes and erotic nymphs. It is as though the sculptors had tried to incorporate the whole spectrum of Indian culture into their work. They seem to have succeeded; Indians, at least, thought of their temples as replicas of the entire universe in stone.

A PROFUSION OF CARVING *embellishes the capital of a stone column and a lintel inside a Buddhist cave-temple at Ajanta. From the lintel, stone ribbing springs upward along a vaulted ceiling.*

A BUDDHIST SANCTUARY CARVED FROM LIVING ROCK

India's oldest surviving examples of religious architecture are not really buildings at all, but man-made caverns hollowed out of mountainsides. The first ones were excavated during the Third Century B.C. by Buddhist monks, who traditionally lived in grottoes in the hills. These cave-temples reached their fullest development more than five centuries later during the artistic flowering of the Gupta Empire. Among the most elaborate examples is the 68-foot-long sanctuary shown here, one of 30 Buddhist temples and monastic halls carved into the remote hills of Ajanta in Hyderabad.

At the heart of the temple (*below, right*) is a domed stupa, a replica of the earliest Buddhist monuments, whose hemispherical tops symbolized the dome of the heavens. The Buddha's enlightenment was periodically celebrated by a procession of monks, who walked around the stupa chanting scriptures. But not all the temple's features are strictly Buddhist. The sumptuously carved pillars and the arched ribs of the vaulted ceiling are stone approximations of the wooden columns and beams of India's earliest jungle shrines, whose very timbers were believed to contain the spirits of the gods.

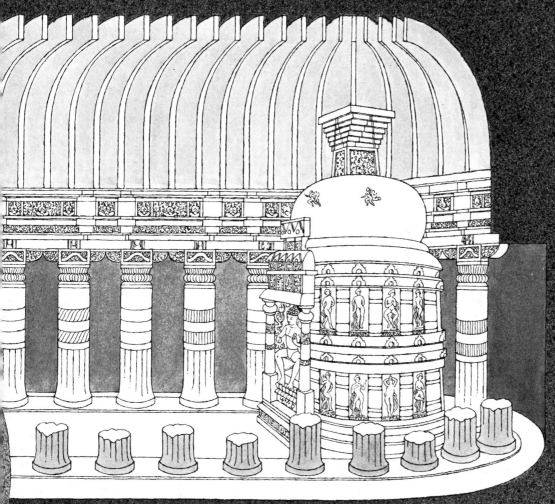

A CLIFFSIDE PRAYER HALL, *its interior shown in a cutaway drawing, was carved out of the rock at Ajanta in the Seventh Century. The stupa at right is embellished with Buddhist statuary.*

AN EARLY SANCTUARY *at Bhuvaneshvar, dating from 750 A.D., shows a fairly simple, clear-cut design in this comparative-scale drawing. Its 44-foot tower is flanked by a rectangular hall with a flat roof.*

A LATER SHRINE, *the small Mukteswar Temple was erected two centuries after the building at the left; its design is more complex and ornate, with carved pilasters and a pyramidal roof over its entrance hall.*

ORNATE TEMPLE-TOWERS INSPIRED BY HINDU FAITH

An upsurge of Hinduism during the last days of the Gupta Empire brought the Indian temple above ground and into a more elaborate stage of development. Thousands of shrines were built, each dedicated to a particular Hindu god. In one of the largest concentrations, at Bhuvaneshvar, near India's eastern coast, 700 temples were erected along the shore of a sacred lake. The older ones, which date from the Eighth Century, are simple two-room shrines, modest in size and restrained in ornament. But with time, the temples grew into multichambered complexes like the structure at

the right, endowed with lofty, beehive-shaped towers and completely covered by extravagant carvings.

Like their Buddhist predecessors, the Hindu temples carried a symbolic meaning in almost every element of their design. An inner sanctum, housing a replica of the temple's deity, was built in the form of a square, the imagined shape of the universe. Above this soared the tallest of the temple's spires, which was intended to represent several different Hindu concepts: the mountain of Shiva, Universal Man or a mythological pillar connecting heaven and earth.

A SERIES OF SPACES, *increasing in height from the entrance at far left, leads to the tiny inner sanctum of the Lingaraja Temple, shown at the base of the tallest spire in the cutaway drawing below. The largest and most elaborate building at Bhuvaneshvar, the temple was erected around 1000 A.D.*

PATTERNS AND FIGURES *cover a wall of a temple at Bhuvaneshvar (left). A dwarf and a dancing girl embellish two pilasters. The stylized strings of beads at far left stand for the eternal flowing of the earth's waters.*

A DECORATIVE MAIDEN *from the Rajarani Temple at Bhuvaneshvar is thought to represent either a dancing girl in the retinue of one of the Hindu gods, or a goddess derived from an early Indian folk religion.*

A WEALTH OF SCULPTURE TO SHOW A RICH MYTHOLOGY

Much of the increasing flamboyance of Hindu temples resulted from sheer love of carved ornament. Not a single exterior surface of the Bhuvaneshvar shrines was left untouched by the sculptor's hand. Stone nymphs, demons, serpents, dwarfs and dancing girls cavort among the nooks and pilasters that form the temples' façades. Many of the figures are taken from Hindu mythology, and include representations of Shiva, Vishnu and other Hindu gods with their attendant spirits. Other motifs, such as figures of lions and crocodile-like monsters, were borrowed from the Buddhists.

Still other carvings were derived from Indian folk religions, and include the tree-spirits and fertility figures worshiped in pre-Hindu times by the Dravidians.

One reason for the great quantity of sculpture was the didactic character of Hinduism: the builders of the temples were trying to make clear to the worshipers, who were often illiterate, the intricate mythology of their faith. Another reason stems from one of the rituals of Hinduism, in which the creation of religious art, accompanied by the proper incantations, was itself considered an act of worship.

A COLOSSAL "CHARIOT" FOR A MIGHTY SUN-GOD

While hundreds of carvings served as decoration on most Indian temples, the entire Temple of the Sun at Konarak was conceived as a single piece of sculpture. Built around 1250 A.D., Konarak preserved the pineapple-shaped tower and square entrance hall found at Bhuvaneshvar. But the architect also thought of his design as an enormous replica of the sun-god's cosmic chariot. Around its base, he placed 12 huge wheels. Along the front staircase he had carved seven mighty horses (partially visible at left in the picture below) to pull the solar vehicle across the sky.

Unfortunately, the architect's full ambitions were never realized. The tower, which would have measured some 225 feet in height, one of the largest in India, collapsed before it could be completed; its probable shape, deduced from designs used in similar temples, is drawn below.

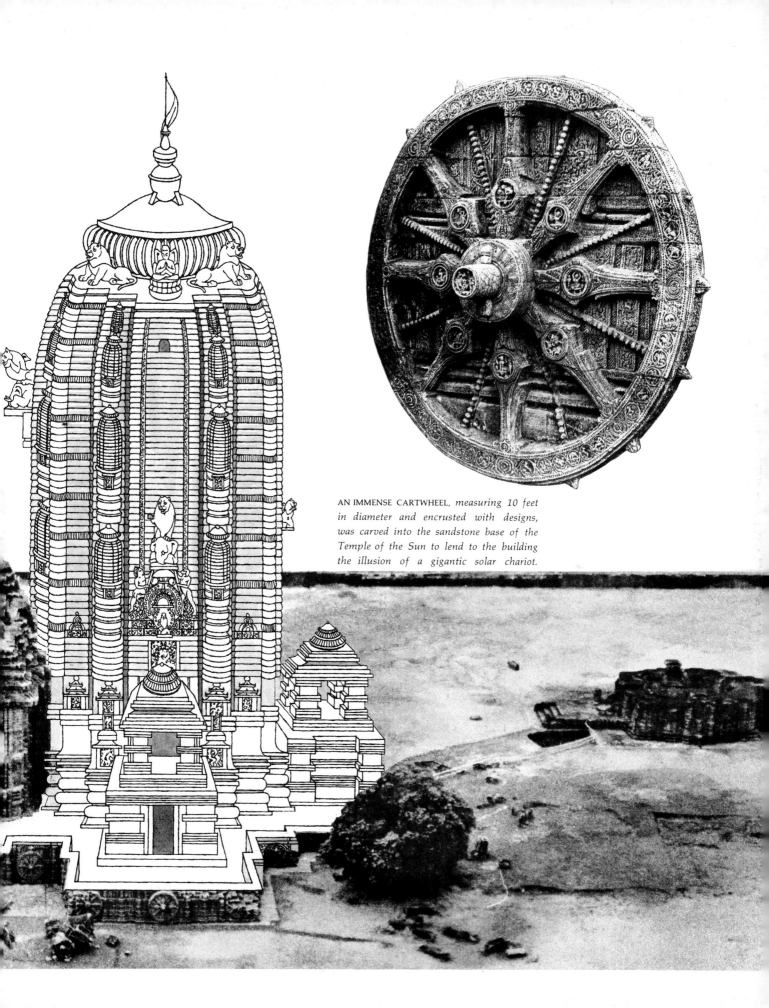

AN IMMENSE CARTWHEEL, *measuring 10 feet in diameter and encrusted with designs, was carved into the sandstone base of the Temple of the Sun to lend to the building the illusion of a gigantic solar chariot.*

A "MOUNTAIN OF SNOW" AND ITS SULTRY CARVINGS

In the 10th Century A.D., a minor prince of central India adorned his capital, Khajuraho, with what has been described as "a charming, splendid home of Vishnu which rivals the peaks of the mountain of snow." The building was one of 20 temples at Khajuraho, a city that contained some of the most graceful works of Hindu architecture.

Although the Khajuraho shrines are smaller than the grandiose monuments of Bhuvaneshvar and Konarak, they give an even greater impression of soaring height. Each temple is raised more than 20 feet above the ground on a lofty terrace; its various halls and pavilions are compressed into a compact shape, in which domed spires strain upward like a succession of foothills toward a mountainous main tower. The temples, in fact, are symbolic replicas of a Himalayan peak where the gods were believed to dwell.

Carved into the temple walls are sculptures that suggest the delights of living in the home of the gods. Many of these works depict voluptuous maidens and amorous couples. Some are brazenly erotic, showing the influence of a Hindu concept that imbued sexual pleasure with divine qualities.

SENSUOUS BEAUTIES *crowd the façade of the Devi Jagadambi Temple at Khajuraho. The temple reflects the beliefs of the Tantric cult of Hinduism, which celebrated the sexual union of man and woman as being symbolic of the union of earthly beings with the divine.*

THE MOUNTAINOUS EFFECT *of the Kandariya Mahadeo Temple (opposite page) is enhanced by its compact design and series of aspiring domes. The floor plan of a sister temple (bottom) shows how pavilions and halls have been merged into a single, integrated structure.*

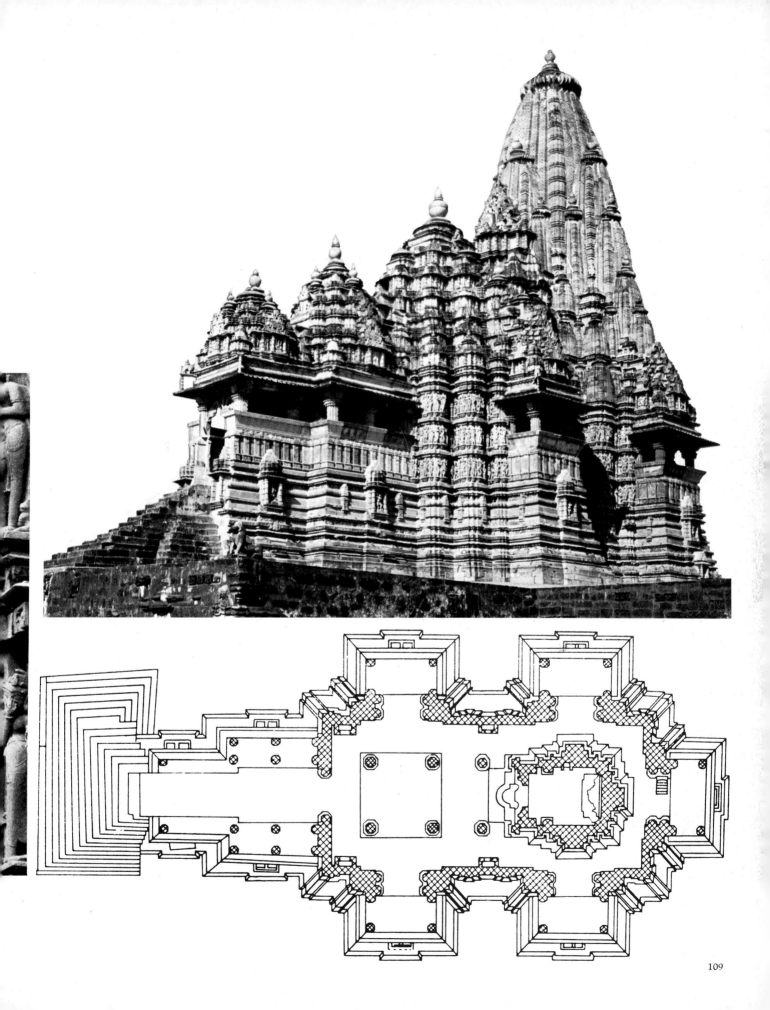

TEMPLES THAT BECAME CITIES

While the builders in northern India were raising mountainlike shrines, a different type of temple architecture was evolving in the far south. In its own way it was as complex and universal as the styles of northern and central India. Its massive gateways and labyrinthine walls sprawled over many acres and embraced whole communities of religious buildings, as in the 14th Century Arunacalesvara Temple *(right)*, some 100 miles from Madras.

The great southern temples grew up around small sanctuaries that were located in central courtyards and enclosed by heavy stone walls. In time, their precincts were expanded by the addition of concentric rings of newer and larger walls. Gateways developed into monumental rectangular pyramids with 100-foot superstructures of brick, their outer surfaces entirely smothered in stucco carvings of gods and fanciful beasts.

Often the expanding temples grew to encompass entire towns. Merchants set up bazaars in the shadow of pillared halls built for religious festivals. Children scurried among the shrines and dormitories erected for pilgrims, and men and women performed ritual ablutions in huge stone pools. Within the walls of these temple cities the mystical religion of the Hindu priests was merged completely with the bustling vitality of daily life.

6

THE FLOWERING
OF HINDUISM

Between the Fifth Century B.C. and the Fourth Century A.D., India brought into flower the great devotional religion of Hinduism. It is unlike any Western faith. It has gods that number in the millions, any of whom—from all to one or none—may be adored with equal propriety. It has no fixed system of worship: some Hindus pray, others meditate, others make sacrifices. It has no single prophet who codified and evangelized its beliefs; rather it developed from the primitive worship of the forces of nature and the Vedic philosophy of India's dim past. And yet underlying this strange assemblage of ideas and holy figures, combined and transmuted from several beginnings, is a solid foundation of commonly held belief to unify the diversity that is India.

In its very variety lay Hinduism's strength. By accommodating all classes, all intellects, all personalities, it became even more than a religion; it established the framework for the uniquely Indian society, in which people of widely varying backgrounds, beliefs, social standing and education go their own separate ways—together.

This great faculty for accommodating diverse inclinations caused Hinduism eventually to prevail over Buddhism in India. Early in the Christian era Buddhism reached its peak; then it began to wither in the soil from which it had sprung, as Christianity was to do, and take root abroad instead. For one thing, the brahman class had always led the social organization and intellectual life of India, even while Buddhism was in its ascendancy; given time, the brahmans reasserted themselves in the sphere of religion. In doing so they took advantage of the spirit of pre-Aryan India, which had never fully died out. Even before the rise of Buddhism, when the brahman philosophers were devising the concept of an impersonal world spirit that reigned supreme, the people at large continued to cherish the old gods that antedated the Aryan invaders. In time the brahmans found a way to accommodate the gods of the people with the brahman scriptures, the Vedas, and with the commentaries on them, the Upanishads, and with Buddhism as well. This reconciliation of worship, philosophy and ethical behavior produced Hinduism.

By the Fourth Century A.D. Hinduism had

A GOD OF MANY QUALITIES, *Shiva grasps in two of his hands emblems of his diverse nature: the drum of creation and the flame of destruction. The dwarf under his foot represents the illusions that Shiva dispels.*

conceived the themes that make it what it is today. It went on from that time to expand, as it continues to do; but the essential principles had been laid, the principles on which its further growth was to depend. The Hindus had produced philosophers of extraordinary insight; they had established a pantheon of rich diversity; they had developed a comforting form of popular worship; they had written a great literature that nourished and taught the people.

Hinduism was then, as it is today, a multifarious and elusive complex. Together the Hindus have but one article of faith in common: that man will work out his destiny through the interaction of karma (the law of cause and effect that determines his station in life), dharma (the duties incumbent upon him in that station) and reincarnation (rebirth in another life). This theme is basic to all interpretations of the character, actions and meaning of the Hindu gods.

Of the millions of deities in the pantheon, five stand out, and most Hindus worship only one; they generally regard the millions of gods simply as different manifestations of the one deity whom they worship. In that respect the many gods are reconciled with Brahman, the supreme being that was conceived three millennia ago in the religious scriptures of the Upanishads. This all-pervading, all-powerful presence is the source from which Hindus derived the god Brahma, who in theory (though not in popularity) is first among the gods.

In modern form, Brahma is more of a god than the impersonal spirit of the Upanishads—he is considered to be masculine, for example—yet he is not quite anthropomorphized into an ideal human figure. His claim to first place in the pantheon rests on his role as creator of the universe. But he is not a creator in the sense of the Old Testament Jehovah, who willed the world into being at a given point in prehistory; rather, he generates a creation

comparable to the renewal of the earth that comes repeatedly, like spring. Two other deities regulate this cosmic renewal process: Shiva, who destroys creation, as old age destroys youth and fall destroys the creation of spring; and Vishnu, who preserves the universe that Brahma has created, as life is preserved in fallow land or dry seeds. Although Vishnu and Shiva have abstract and impersonal functions like Brahma, they also have human attributes, which he does not. In their anthropomorphic roles they have become the most popular Hindu gods, exciting intense sects whose devotees worship their particular deity as a monotheistic god who grants or denies salvation.

Ranking behind Vishnu and Shiva in popularity, appearing now in the role of the latter's wife, now as the object of a cult in her own right, is a mother goddess called by several names—Kali, Durga, Parvati, and Uma among them. She is a new version of the mother goddess common to ancient societies; such a goddess was worshiped in the Indus Valley before the arrival of the Aryans. Finally, there is the fifth of the important Hindu gods, Krishna, one of several human incarnations of Vishnu.

The concepts that these gods and their lesser companions represent can all be traced back to the Vedic Age and even before. The Vedas told that Vishnu took three giant steps by which he measured out the universe, then set it in motion and kept it going—a function he still performs as God the Preserver. But the Vedas gave no hint of the importance Vishnu was ultimately to have, for only six of the thousand Vedic hymns are devoted to him. He ascended in importance, however, with the receding of Indra, the early war-god and patron of the Aryans—probably a phenomenon that occurred as the conquering Aryans settled down in India, and the distinctions between conquerors and vanquished blurred. As Vishnu rose in importance and popularity, he took on various characteristics

THE ARYAN GOD OF WAR, *Indra, seen riding an elephant and brandishing daggers, was considered king of heaven in early times. Later Hindus gave Indra a lower status, but they continued to worship him as ruler of the skies and god of rain and thunder.*

of the fading Indra—most notably his martial instincts and his love of worldly pleasures.

But bellicosity in Vishnu is offset by a primarily benevolent nature; he is essentially a god of compassion and mercy. When man gets himself in trouble, Vishnu appears on earth to help mankind. He is said to have had a number of incarnations in history, and many Hindus expect more to come. Some Hindus credit the Buddha as an incarnation of Vishnu, some accept Jesus as one, and all lovers of the great epic literature of India see its heroes as the god Vishnu in human guise.

The best-known, best-loved and most complex of Vishnu's manifestations is that of Krishna, who figures in a host of legends. The myths tell that he was born in a palace prison, where his mother had been confined because the king's seers had predicted that a child of his clan would slay the king. Mother and child escape, however, as they do in the similar legend surrounding Perseus in Greece;

and the king—echoing now the deed of the Biblical Herod—orders the slaying of all male children in the realm. Again the infant god foils the plot; he finds haven in the country, where, like Oedipus, he is brought up by a herdsman and his wife. As a child he is incorrigibly mischievous, but he more than atones for his pranks by slaying demons and miraculously saving the cowherds from calamity. As a youth he is irresistible; he courts and wins the love of countless peasant girls. Later he turns solemn and goes to war—and fulfills the prophecy of the seers by killing the king. He marries more than 16,000 wives, who bear him 180,000 sons. He founds his own kingdom—which, like the Greek Atlantis, is eventually swallowed by the sea. According to one legend, reminiscent of the Greek myth of Achilles, he dies when an arrow strikes his one vulnerable spot, his heel.

If Vishnu figures only slightly in the early Vedic literature, Shiva figures not at all—not, at least, by name. But of all the gods in India, he is among the oldest in origins, for his attributes combine those of at least three ancient deities—a Harappan fertility-god (whom the conquering Aryans had scorned), the ethical Varuna, who in the Vedas guarded the cosmic law, and finally Rudra, a wrathful Jehovah-like titan who in the Vedas punished and destroyed wrongdoers and anyone else that roused his displeasure. As the modern Shiva he is simultaneously the god of mystical stillness and the god of dance; the god of bounty and the god of wrath; the god of destruction and the god of fertility—a mythical acknowledgment of the fact that everything that comes to birth comes ultimately to death, and from death comes new life. He is cruel and tender, wrathful and merciful, unpredictable and ever the same. He is an ascetic who sits in towering meditation on the Himalayan Mount Kailas; he is also a reveler, a drunken Bacchus who thunders down the mountainside, dancing the world to destruction as he goes. Insofar as he punishes evil, he is moral; more often he is as impersonal as nature, inflicting terror and grief for no apparent reason. Yet despite his fearful aspects, Shiva evokes the intensest adoration from his devotees, for he fascinates even as he terrifies.

Some of Shiva's worshipers believe his driving power comes not from himself but from a feminine spirit called his *shakti*—his wife. Such worshipers belong to the so-called *shakta* cults, those that adore Shiva's wife in various manifestations.

Shiva's wife, like himself, is a composite of ancient and contradictory deities. She is kind and cruel, fearsome and beautiful; as a mother-goddess she has a hand in creation, but she feeds on blood. In her kindly aspects she is known as Parvati (meaning "Daughter of the Mountain") or Uma ("Light"); in her dreadful aspects she is Kali (the "Black One") or Durga (the "Inaccessible"). She has a score of other names as well. When she emerged as Shiva's wife, about the Fourth Century A.D., she gathered other goddesses into the pantheon with her, though few of them acquired her status. Vishnu took as a wife Lakshmi, the goddess of luck—a deity who, like the Greek Aphrodite, rose full blown out of the sea. Together with her husband she has had frequent incarnations—she is Radha, the favorite peasant girl of Krishna's philandering youth; she is Rukmini, chief queen of Krishna's 16,000 wives; she is Sita, the constant wife of Rama, hero of the epic called the *Ramayana*.

The characters of the gods and the ideas of Hinduism are developed in the great body of classic Indian literature, much of which is religious in intent or interpretation. The Vedas and the Upanishads are only part of this literature. Chief among the others are two epics—the *Mahabharata*, or "Great War," and the *Ramayana*, or "Story of Rama." They are at once heroic tales and moral lessons; on the one hand, they extol the deeds of antiquity, and on the other they have for Hindus a religious meaning so vital that they are revered as Biblical stories are in the West. As heroic tales they correspond to the *Iliad* and the *Odyssey* of ancient Greece: the *Mahabharata* is a tale of war, in which the gods fight side by side with mortals; the *Ramayana* is the tale of an exile and his patient, faithful wife. Like the *Iliad* and the *Odyssey*—like the folklore of all peoples—the *Mahabharata* and the *Ramayana* represent thousands of years of folk memory, and probably spring from a grain of historical truth. In their idealization of man and his virtues, and their insight into the universal human condition, they rank as great world literature.

The *Ramayana* begins as the tale of a golden age in the kingdom of Ayodhya, a time when

> Rich in royal worth and valor,
>   rich in holy Vedic lore,
> Dasaratha ruled his empire
>   in the happy days of yore. . . .

Peaceful lived the righteous people,
rich in wealth, in merit high;
Envy dwelt not in their bosoms,
and their accents shaped no lie.

Fathers with their happy households
owned their cattle, corn and gold;
Galling penury and famine
in Ayodhya had no hold.

But affairs take a sorry turn when the jealous stepmother of the Crown Prince Rama reminds the king that he once promised her any favor she might ask. She wants Rama exiled; she has a son of her own for whom she covets the throne. Rama is a man of consummate honor, the soul of the Indian concept of dharma. Though his kin and countrymen beg him to stay, his dharma—that is, his sense of duty—and his respect for his elders require that he abide by his father's promise. Without a word of reproach, he prepares to set off. Such a prince, of course, must have a flawless wife, and Rama has one in Sita, a princess from a neighboring kingdom. She might have returned to her father's palace; instead she accompanies Rama into exile.

Rama and Sita go to live in a forest hut, where they lead an ascetic life—an existence that is held in high esteem by Hindus. Rama interrupts his meditations now and then to slay demons that abound in the woods, arousing the wrath of Ravana, the king of the demons. This evil creature, seeking revenge on Rama, steals into the prince's hut one day, abducts Sita and carries her off to his castle, where he does all in his power to win her affection. He has no luck; the faithful Sita resists his lures and remains true to Rama.

Rama, meanwhile, has not been idle; with the help of the gods he has raised a band of fighting men and an army of sacred monkeys. After a long search, they come upon Ravana's hideaway and rescue Sita. But finding his bride, Rama faces a di-

lemma. Being in love with her, he wants to take her back, but being bound by sacred law, he must cast her out for having lived under another man's roof. Sita does as her dharma demands; she throws herself onto a funeral pyre. But because she is innocent, the fire-god Agni refuses to take her, and she comes out of the fire unscathed. With this proof of her virtue, Rama takes her back.

When eventually he reinherits his rightful kingdom from his half-brother, who generously abdicates in his favor, his people receive his return with rejoicing. But after a time they begin to whisper about his wife. How can a woman who has dallied with another man properly reign as Rama's queen? So Rama, whose first duty is to please his subjects, sadly decides for the second time to send her away —and now no god like Agni comes to her defense. Rama rules without her for several years, then has a change of heart, and asks her back. But he has waited too long; Sita has been swallowed up by the earth of which she was born. Rama spends the rest of his days sad and alone, but a great hero for the noble spirit with which he executes his dharma.

The epic tale of Rama and Sita was composed about the Third Century B.C. In time, Rama came to stand for the model Hindu—he is chivalrous and devoted to his wife, but obedient to sacred law; he has forbearance in tribulation, but courage in adversity. Eventually he came to be seen as an incarnation of Vishnu, and his name is sometimes used as a synonym for God. Sita evolved with him. In her fidelity to Rama and her obedience to dharma, she stands for the divine ideal of the Hindu wife. And, as he is the god Vishnu, so she is an incarnation of Vishnu's wife, Lakshmi.

The *Ramayana* has been told and retold for more than 2,000 years, until it is deep in the bones of all Hindus. It provides more than entertainment for the people. Like the folklore of every civilization, it expresses the ideals dearest to the hearts of the culture that spawned it—ideals that are meant to be applied to daily life. The Hindu bride, for instance, cherishes the words that Sita spoke when she was about to follow Rama into exile:

> Car and steed and gilded palace,
>   vain are these to woman's life;
> Dearer is her husband's shadow
>   to the loved and loving wife.
> Happier than in father's mansions,
>   in the woods will Sita rove,
> Waste no thought on home or kindred,
>   nestling in her husband's love. . . .
> And the wild fruit she will gather
>   from the fresh and fragrant wood,
> And the food by Rama tasted
>   shall be Sita's cherished food.

And as the mythology of Greece and Rome has fed the arts of the West to the present day, so the *Ramayana* has fed the arts of India; Rama, Sita and their fellow-characters have figured again and again in the prose and poetry, painting and sculpture, dance and song that India has produced throughout her long history.

Equally influential, and more profound, is the other epic, the *Mahabharata*, which, like the *Ramayana*, is part heroic tale, part religious lesson. The *Mahabharata* tells the story of a bloody war fought for a kingdom—and the tale is probably a semihistorical account of an internecine struggle that took place north of Delhi at the dawn of the First Millennium B.C.

As the *Mahabharata* has it, the throne of the Kuru tribe had fallen to a blind prince, who because of his affliction was barred by law from ruling. He therefore ceded the throne to his younger brother Pandu. The trouble begins when their sons reach maturity. By law the crown should next devolve to Yudhisthira, the eldest son of Pandu; but the blind man's sons understandably want for

A MANY-ARMED GOD OF FURY *stabs an enemy demon in this detail from a Hindu temple sculpture in southern India. Hindu sculptors considered a deity's arms to be extensions of his inner energy and the objects in his hands to be symbolic of his various cosmic powers.*

themselves the kingdom that they might have had but for their father's blindness. The eldest of them challenges Yudhisthira to a game of dice; he cheats and wins the kingdom for himself, but, subsequently persuaded to compromise, he agrees to return the throne to Yudhisthira after a period of 13 years.

The 13 years pass and Yudhisthira reclaims the throne, but his cousin has learned to like the taste of power and goes back on his promise. So Yudhisthira and his brothers go to war—reluctantly, because they are peace-loving men and their cousins have been their lifelong friends—and in a bloody struggle that lasts for 18 days, all their cousins are killed. Yudhisthira and his brothers win the war and the kingdom, and Yudhisthira rules wisely into his old age.

This grim tale of war is the vehicle for expounding on all manner of Indian ideas: on Krishna as an incarnation of the god Vishnu; on dharma, particularly as it applies to royalty; on love and grief and caste. In the middle of the account of the battle, the *Mahabharata* has a separate segment of some 700 couplets that stands alone as an independent religious treatise and work of art. This is the *Bhagavad Gita*, or "Lord's Song"; and so sacred is it to Hindus that it corresponds to the New Testament in the Christian world. The *Bhagavad Gita* is a sermon given by the god Krishna to Arjuna, a younger brother of Yudhisthira. The prince, who quails at killing his relatives, cries out to the god, who has joined the war and is serving as Arjuna's charioteer:

Krishna! As I behold, come here to shed
Their common blood, you concourse of our kin,
My members fail, my tongue dries in my mouth. . . .
It is not good, O [Krishna]! Naught of good
Can spring from mutual slaughter! Lo, I hate
Triumph and domination, wealth and ease

Thus sadly won! Alas, what victory
Can bring delight [O Krishna], what rich spoils
Could profit, what rule recompense, what span
Of life itself seem sweet, bought with such blood?

But Krishna has not joined the battle for nothing. "Let them perish, Prince, and fight!" he exclaims. This cold-blooded counsel the god justifies on three counts. First, the soul cannot be slain because it is eternal; only the body dies. Thus Arjuna cannot really kill his cousins, and besides, he will do them a favor, for in dying they will move out of this life and on to the next. Second, his dharma, or duty as a prince, and therefore a member of the warrior class, is to fight. Third, if he fails to do so, his enemies will accuse him of cowardice. Arjuna is not convinced, so Krishna tells him he cannot win salvation unless he does his duty—that is, unless he fights; and if he does so by detaching his "self" from the act he is committing, he will be like the ascetic for whom "supreme bliss draws nigh."

Perhaps Krishna protests too much. If the poem patently sanctifies dharma as expounded by the brahmans, it just as surely lays bare the failings of the existing order. Yudhisthira, whose kingdom is at stake, is no less unhappy over the war and its inevitable disaster than is his younger brother. "There is nothing more evil than a kshatriya's [warrior's] dharma," he says to Krishna. "Stop this cruel carnage!" he begs. He even goes so far as to curse the concept of dharma.

But more than exposing iniquities peculiar to Hindu society, the *Mahabharata* speaks to the universal human condition; and in this it rises to the level of art. Yudhisthira voices the eternal struggle of individual conscience against society as it is ordered, and he shares the universal plight of man powerless against forces he did not create—forces he may decry but has to reckon with. Like the hero of a Greek tragedy, Yudhisthira is a noble figure

DISTINCTIVE HEAD MARKINGS *identify the followers of the two largest sects of Hinduism. Shaivites, who worship the god Shiva, paint bands across their foreheads (far left). Vaishnavites, adherents of Vishnu, wear three vertical lines (left).*

who is punished in the end for one failing. On reaching the city of the gods after his death, he finds his vain and pompous cousin, whose greed had brought on the war, feasting happily among the gods. Then, like Dante, he is escorted on a tour of hell, where he endures the sight of his brothers and his wife burning in a pit. He cries out in anguish, only to hear from the gods that his cousin had earned his reward by fulfilling his dharma in going to war without quailing. Yudhisthira himself, for cursing the gods and questioning dharma, is condemned to a stint in hell and further rebirth, in order that he may work out his dharma better.

In other passages the *Bhagavad Gita* reaffirms the Hindu desire for reconciliation of all things in one. At one point Krishna declares to Arjuna:

> *Gaze [upon me]. I manifest for thee*
> *Those hundred thousand thousand shapes that*
> *clothe my Mystery.*
> *I show thee all my semblances, infinite, rich,*
> *divine,*

> *My changeful hues, my countless forms. See!*
> *in this face of mine . . .*
> *Wonders unnumbered, Indian Prince! . . .*
> *Behold! This is the universe!*

This is an extension of the thesis stated in the Upanishads that everything in the universe is one with everything else; that appearances ("those hundred thousand shapes") are illusion; they "clothe" the "mystery" of the one true Reality.

But even as he reaffirms the ancient concept of oneness, Krishna reveals a shift in the concept of god and of man's relation to him. God, or the prevailing spirit behind the universe, remains one with creation, but he is no longer impassive; he is a personal god who loves man, who desires love in return and—most significant—he is a god who will assist man in his course through life. Not only is this implicit in the appearance of the god Krishna at Arjuna's side in battle; lest the point be missed, the god tells Arjuna in no uncertain terms at the close of his exhortation:

120

Take my last word, my utmost meaning have!
Precious thou art to me; right well-beloved!
Listen! I tell thee for thy comfort this.
Give me thy heart! adore me! serve me! cling
In faith and love and reverence to me!
So shalt thou come to me! I promise true,
For thou art sweet to me! . . . Fly to me alone!
Make me thy single refuge! I will free
Thy soul from all its sins!

Such a god as Krishna is a far remove from Brahman, the impersonal world spirit put forth in the Upanishads. Krishna's words indicate how the concept of the deity had evolved. By the Fourth Century A.D. the loving kind of deity of which he spoke had grasped the hearts of the people—and as it took hold there arose a new form of worship appropriate to such a god. The worship was *bhakti*—from the Sanskrit word *bhaj*, the original meaning of which was "to share or participate in"; *bhakti* is a form of intense personal devotion. Practically any or all of India's manifold deities may be the object of *bhakti*; but in practice the gods Vishnu, Shiva and Shiva's wife in several guises get the lion's share of it.

But even as popular devotion to a personal deity grew, philosophic speculation never ceased. Far from ignoring or condemning devotion to the gods, the brahmans not only sanctioned it but participated in it as well. They still treasured the Upanishads as sacred scripture, but they sought to absorb the new deities into an ever-expanding philosophical scheme. Continuing the tradition begun in the Vedic age, philosophers all over India went on debating the secrets of the universe, seeking always to find unity in the multiplicity of the world around them.

Of all the philosophers that India has produced, one who graced the Ninth Century A.D. ranks among the great minds in all history. That was Shankara, a brahman born in Kerala, in southern India. In a brief life of 32 years he did for Hinduism what the 13th Century Thomas Aquinas did for Christianity: he took his religion apart and examined it in minute detail, then drew the pieces together again in one cohesive whole. He wrote the most famous of all the commentaries on the Upanishads and established himself as chief exponent of the system of philosophy most esteemed by Hindu intellectuals.

Like many philosophers and all great men, Shankara was a host of human contradictions. He discarded the concept of a warm and loving deity in favor of the ancient impersonal Brahman of the Upanishads, but he persisted in writing eloquent hymns in praise of Shiva. He had no use for the Buddhists, but he employed missionary techniques similar to theirs. He dismissed reason as inferior to intuition, yet his achievement rests essentially upon his brilliance in dialectics.

Like Thomas Aquinas, Shankara accepted without question the scriptures of his religion as divine revelation, then dared to set about verifying them through the use of reason. Having done that much, he parts company with his Christian counterpart, for Aquinas, although he left much that was unexplainable to be accepted on faith, never doubted the power of reason. Shankara, on the contrary, professed to abandon reason in the end, declaring that intuition—the ability to seize on truth without recourse to reason—is more to be prized than reason itself. All knowledge, he said, is warped and inconclusive, for the senses impair man's grasp of reality. Hampered by illusion and ignorance, man sees many forms where there is in truth only one reality—Brahman: a reality that is changeless, timeless and unified in all things. Only through the practice of asceticism, and through the ascetic control of the senses, can man attain salvation; and in Shankara's philosophy salvation does not mean "union" of the soul with Brahman, but rather absorption in it through the intuitive grasp of the truth that the soul and Brahman are one. When man achieves that insight he will be able to quit the cycle of rebirths forever.

Shankara's statements about the soul and Brahman were not new; they merely reaffirmed the concepts set forth in the Upanishads more than a thousand years before his time. Neither was his advocacy of asceticism original; insofar as it meant a life of austerity, a giving up of worldly goods and pleasures, asceticism was a time-honored tradition in India. What was new was his systematic arrangement of the diffuse concepts of the Upanishads. What modern philosophers are able to discern in the obscurities and self-contradictions of the ancient scriptures, they see largely through Shankara's elucidation of them.

Not everyone, of course, is suitably equipped for the practice of asceticism, nor endowed with insight; and Shankara conceded that for lesser mortals salvation may come through worship of Shiva, Vishnu or any other god of the pantheon one chooses. But those gods, like the illusions of self, are in the last analysis merely half-way manifestations of the ultimate spirit, Brahman; they are necessary only so long as man is hampered by illusion and ignorance. The highest salvation is reserved for those who take the arduous path of asceticism; only in that way can they master their senses and then pierce through illusion to reach the goal of insight.

Shankara's philosophy, like that of the Upanishads on which he based it, was fine for those with the intellectual mettle to grasp it and live by it. But the average Indian could no more reach Shankara's heights than he could plumb the secrets of the Vedas. Bhakti prevailed over ascetic meditation—and not among the peasants alone, but in all strata of society throughout India. It remained for another philosopher in the 11th Century—Ramanuja, also a southern brahman—to give to the practice of bhakti the blessing of philosophical formulation.

Like every Hindu philosopher who had preceded him, Ramanuja retained the concepts of dharma, karma and reincarnation—virtually the only ideas of Hinduism never to have been abandoned—but unlike most of his predecessors, he rated ascetic meditation second to devotional worship, and argued the merits of a truly personal deity over the impassive Brahman. Shankara had allowed devotion to a personal god as the means to an end; Ramanuja extolled it as an end in itself. Shankara saw the soul as identical with Brahman and the goal of life as absorption of the one in the other; Ramanuja saw the soul and god as separate entities, and the goal of life as communion of the two. Shankara put the burden of salvation on man himself; Ramanuja gave the deity a role in the process. In words that could have come from the Psalms of David or a Christian litany, he described his god— Vishnu—as an "ocean of tenderness," a sublimely merciful spirit who "takes away [man's] sorrows." The idea of such a bountiful supreme spirit had lain for centuries in Krishna's discourse to Arjuna, but Ramanuja was the first to articulate it as formal philosophy.

The musings of a philosopher such as Shankara or Ramanuja may be little known to the peasant who worships at a shrine; they may indeed be beyond his reach. But civilization flowers when the intellectual flights of the one correspond to the unarticulated feelings that beat in the breast of the other. In their ceaseless questing after unity in multiplicity, Indian philosophers from the Vedic Age onward forged for themselves and their people such a reconciliation in Hinduism. It is no coincidence that the centuries in which the Hindu religion was developing in complexity were also the centuries of India's greatest development in culture —in the arts, in economics, in statecraft.

KNEELING HUMBLY, *the four-headed god Brahma salutes Krishna in a pasture where Krishna and his companions have been grazing their herd of cattle.*

A GOD FOR ALL SEASONS

From its beginning in India some 1,500 years before Christ, Hinduism was remarkable for its ability to assimilate all ideas and to attract all men. No divinity exerted this appeal more than Krishna, a god famed for love of humanity. His devotees regarded him as an incarnation of Vishnu, the god who protected men from destruction and sustained order in the world. What made Krishna popular, however, was not so much his divine lineage as the fact that legends portrayed him as intensely human. As a baby he was as naughty as any ordinary infant, and it was Krishna as a child that the mothers of India adored. Young men admired Krishna the adolescent, who worked as a cowherd and won glory in battle; girls, in turn, revered him as a passionate lover. For centuries Krishna's cult was so widespread that India's finest artists labored to illustrate his story, and his worshipers found it quite natural that even Brahma, the creator of the universe, should bow *(above)* before the charming, handsome god.

A PRECOCIOUS MISCHIEF-MAKER

In the tales of his childhood, Krishna was depicted as a devilish boy who differed from other children only in his great strength and good looks. (Artists added to these distinctions by painting his skin blue, recalling the fact that he was an incarnation of Vishnu, who was symbolically associated with that color.)

One day, the story goes, little Krishna stole some butter from a pot *(above)*. His mother discovered the pilfering and punished the boy by tying him to a heavy mortar used for pulverizing food. Growing restless, Krishna exerted his superhuman strength, dragged the mortar between two trees and casually uprooted them. The noise brought the boy's family and neighbors outside to look *(right)*. There they were surprised to see two princes, who long ago had been imprisoned within the trees by a wizard, thanking a slightly bored-looking Krishna for freeing them.

A SLAYER OF MONSTROUS DEMONS

Krishna's progenitor Vishnu was worshiped by the Indians as the preserver of life, and it was believed he came to earth in mortal guise whenever human happiness was jeopardized. Each of Vishnu's incarnations, or avatars, destroyed evil by battling a different demon; as one of these avatars, Krishna was given the duty of ridding the world of a particularly belligerent demon named Kansa.

But Kansa, legendary ruler of a kingdom in northern India, knew of Krishna's mission and sought to destroy him before he could grow up and carry out his task. Kansa commanded one of his monstrous creatures, a giant crane, to surprise and devour young Krishna while the boy was tending a herd of cows. The bird snapped Krishna into his beak *(near right)*; but before it could swallow him, Krishna magically caused his own body to become so hot the crane was forced to drop him. Then, while other cowherds beat the bird with sticks, Krishna split its beak *(center)* and killed it. This ended one round, but there would be many other challenges from Kansa—and from Krishna's rival gods —before he could return to complete the defeat of the demon and his horde.

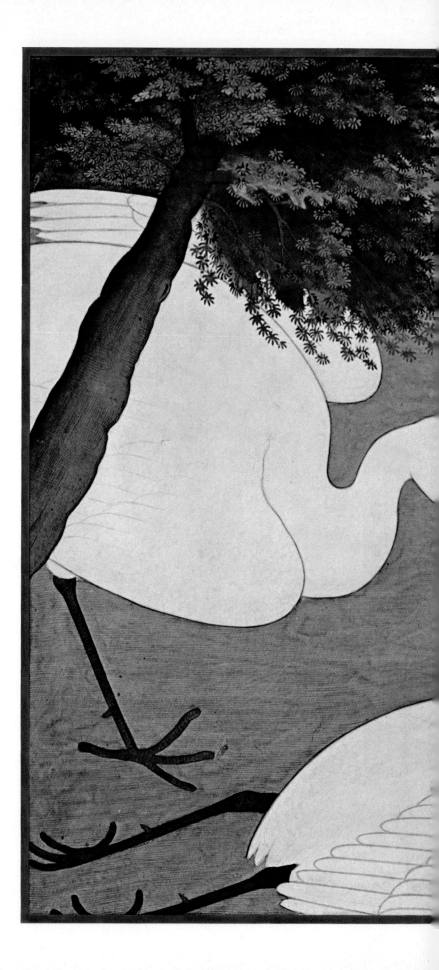

A CHALLENGER OF ANCIENT GODS

As Krishna's triumphs multiplied and his cult spread throughout India, it gradually superseded the worship of many of the older deities. The conflict between the new cult and the old ones was reflected in symbolic tales of Krishna's struggles with these ancient divinities.

One vivid legend symbolized the triumph of the Krishna cult over the worship of Agni, the god of fire. In this tale, Agni, who resented Krishna's popularity among the cowherds, created a forest fire to kill them and their cows one day while they were going to pasture *(above)*. Krishna, however, thwarted Agni with an ancient fire-eating act, sucking up the flames and quenching them in his mouth *(right)*.

A VICTOR OVER THE FORCES OF EVIL

In a final attempt to destroy Krishna, his fated adversary, Kansa invited him to a festival of games. When Krishna accepted, Kansa released a savage elephant upon him, but Krishna killed it. In the arena where the games were to be held, Kansa prepared to watch his wrestlers finish off the god and his brother Balarama. Krishna, however, defeated his man, then observed Balarama win his own match (*below*). Next Krishna seized Kansa himself by the hair, flung him to the earth and killed him (*right*). In this picture the fair-skinned Balarama is seen above Krishna, clubbing Kansa's eight brothers to death. While Krishna's companions, the bare-chested cowherds, anxiously watch the bloody conflict, Kansa's men flee the arena in despair, and the gods express their joy at the evil ruler's defeat by showering petals down from heaven (*background*).

A PASSIONATE LOVER
TO INSPIRE SOULS

Krishna, in addition to all his other attributes, was a man women could not resist. When he played his flute at night, ladies—even respectable married ones—felt helplessly drawn to his side. "Some ran off in the middle of their dinner," one Indian chronicler wrote, "others while bathing and others while engaged in plaiting their hair." Once his admirers had joined him, Krishna would sport with them by moonlight in a forest river *(right)*, lead them in dances and make love to them.

Krishna's love-making was interpreted by Hindus as something far more significant than mere pleasure-seeking. The tales of women abandoning their families to run after him served as poetic expressions of the soul's quest for a union with divinity. Like these inspired women, worshipers of Krishna were expected to neglect all worldly duties to devote themselves single-mindedly to the adoration of the god.

7

CASTE: A PLACE FOR EVERY MAN

If a Hindu pottery maker from a modern Indian village could slip 2,000 years back in time, he would fit into the lives of his remote ancestors with amazing ease. On the mud streets of the ancient village he would see men wearing lengths of white cotton draped exactly like his own *dhoti*. Families squatting outside small wood houses, built like his own house, would be dipping into pottery trays of cooked grain and vegetables soaked in milk—his diet; and flipping the food into their mouths with their fingers—his style of eating. He would find the pottery makers of that distant period—including, perhaps, his own 80-times-removed great-grandfather—shaping bowls and jugs out of moist clay, then baking them in heaps of burning leaves, in just the way that he does today.

What is more important, the 20th Century visitor would also recognize the elaborate code of rights and restrictions guiding the social activities of his ancestors. These social rules dictated the area of a village in which a potter lived, the style in which he dressed, what he ate, when he prayed, whom he married—in short, the pattern of his life from birth to death. The modern villager would not be surprised to find that he and his forefathers had the same occupation and followed the same codes of conduct. Indeed, he would expect it, for both he and those ancestors would be living within the social arrangements known as "caste."

Although this one familiar word can serve to describe India's entire society, caste is far from being as simple or as clear a system as many Westerners believe. In fact, what Westerners have always called caste is actually two different systems: one based on an ideal way of life, the other on a real way of life.

The ideal system consists of a detailed description of the perfect life that brahmans claim was led in the world at the time of creation. It is like a Hindu portrait of a Garden of Eden before sin came into existence, but with Adam and Eve already multiplied into a complete population.

The real way of life in India, however, was much less precise and neat than the brahmans' ideal. It was the system that evolved to give

THE ART OF CRAFTSMAN CASTES, *this gilded medallion set with a turquoise is the work of a silversmith, a goldsmith and a jeweler, each born to his occupation as a member of the hereditary caste devoted to that specialty.*

some order to India's many races, tribes, languages, occupations, religious practices, geographical areas—all the diversity that obtained in such profusion and confusion throughout India's history.

Despite the differences between the ideal system and the actual one, both are based on the age-old Indian concept of dharma. This concept had already been developed by the beginning of the Christian Era—the period to which our potter could return so comfortably. The brahman leaders of India had by then arrived at their great moral principle: that the universe is a harmonious whole only when each of its three component parts—nature, the gods and men—function correctly, fulfilling its dharma, or set of prescribed duties. Nature, for example, performs its duties properly when the three seasons—winter, summer and the rainy season—come and go every year, and when the tides ebb and flow. The gods perform theirs when the great Shiva sits in meditation in his home high on Mount Kailash, and his wife, Parvati, comes to men's aid in the form of the goddess Devi or Kali or Durga. And men perform their duties properly, fulfilling their dharmas, when they follow the customs of the groups they are born into.

In ancient India's bustling towns and villages, each squalling infant grew up knowing that he had to mature in the pattern of his parents. To do so was his dharma; he was never to deviate from tradition. Every act of his life, no matter how trivial, was a religious ritual, enforced as a prescribed duty. The way he brushed his teeth, stepped from his house or greeted his neighbor was supposed to conform to his own group's habits or the universe would tremble. The work he did, the tools he used, the way he used them—his group's ways with all these matters was theoretically part of his dharma, and to tamper with them was to defy the universal order. In this ideal scheme of things, personal inclination was not a major consideration. If a child from a family of cotton merchants liked to nurse sick puppies back to health or to rescue maimed birds and mend their broken wings—signs that, in our own culture, might suggest the family start saving for medical school—his dharma would nevertheless prescribe that he be trained as a merchant. In the words of the *Bhagavad Gita*, "It is better to do one's own duty badly than to do another's duty well," for only when men performed their hereditary dharmas did society function properly as an element of the universe.

To define and codify men's dharmas, brahmans composed elaborate manuals of both ceremonial and everyday behavior. The first books of this kind were collections of aphorisms called sutras, produced as early as the Sixth Century B.C. Gradually, the sections of the sutras concerned with men's everyday duties, the dharma-sutras, were expanded until they became a vast literature in themselves. Around the beginning of the Christian Era, for example, a collection called the *Laws of Manu* was compiled as a complete and authoritative statement of Hindu religious and social codes. In such works, the ideal system—very different from the actual one—can be studied in detail.

According to the *Laws of Manu*, society at the time of creation consisted of four classes of men; men passed through four chronological stages of life; and there were four goals that men were intended to pursue.

The four great classes of the perfect society were strictly graded and segregated. At the top, so high that its members were like divinities, was the class of brahmans. Next came the kshatriya class of kings and warriors. Below them were the vaishyas, or farmers and merchants, and lowest of all were the shudras, or serfs.

Each class had its particular function in the

THE SACRED THREAD, *symbol of an upper-class Hindu's initiation into his caste, is shown draped correctly—across the left shoulder and under the right arm—on a 13th Century sculpture.*

social order. The *Laws of Manu* says that the brahmans were to study and teach the Vedas and to perform sacrifices. Kshatriyas were to protect the people and to study the Vedas. Vaishyas were to breed cattle, till the soil, pursue trade, deal in money—and study the Vedas. Shudras were to serve the other three classes—and were *not* to study the Vedas.

In fact, shudras were forbidden even to read the Vedas. So firm was the ban that the *Laws of Manu* declares that a shudra who hears Vedic verses even accidentally should have molten lead poured in his ears. Such severity reflected a great theoretical difference between the shudra class and the three higher ones. According to this ideal scheme, shudras were born only once. In contrast, brahmans, kshatriyas and vaishyas were "twice-born"—that is, they were born once physically, and born again upon initiation into their class. Only after that second birth was a Hindu con-

sidered a full member of society; theoretically, the shudra was, as one historian puts it, "a second-class citizen, on the fringes of . . . society."

Just as society was divided into the four great classes, so, within the three upper classes, the life of every man was ideally divided into four distinct stages. The stages were those of student, householder, hermit and wanderer.

Student life began at the end of childhood, between the ages of eight and twelve, depending on class. At that point, a boy of the upper classes received the sacred thread of initiation into his class. The triple-strand string, worn throughout his life, announced that he was "twice-born"—a brahman, a kshatriya or a vaishya. After the thread had been ceremoniously placed over his left shoulder and under his right arm, the new student was to leave home—carefully taking the first step with his right foot—and go to live, celibate and attentive, in the house of a guru, or teacher. There the student was supposed to memorize innumerable verses of the Vedas and to master such practical matters as arithmetic, astrology, archery and music. Kshatriya students were to take such additional subjects as fighting, weaponry and the techniques of command.

At the end of the student stage, which could last as long as 12 years, a young man in the perfect society was expected to return home to marry and become a householder. At this stage, he had a series of correct and necessary rituals to perform. Some were special forms of worship, such as a prayerful greeting addressed to the sunrise. Others, equally sacred, might include distributing food to family and guests. In addition to observing such ceremonies, a man in the householder stage of life was obliged to beget sons, in order to make sure that the right way of life lasted beyond his own lifetime.

The third ideal stage of life began after the

householder had seen his son's sons born and thriving. His duty then was to leave the busy world and become a hermit. He could live out this stage of life in back rooms of his own house, leaving his sons to perform the householder's rituals and to take on the full weight of family responsibility. But the sacred literature seems to indicate that, ideally, the hermit retired to a forest hut, either accompanied by his wife or leaving her in the care of his sons. There he was expected to live simply, eating only nuts and fruits, studying the Vedas and treating gently whoever came to him for help or advice. At this stage, a man could become a guru to the children of a new generation.

After a period of calm self-examination and meditation, the hermit was expected to acquire a sense of detachment from the world and its pleasures and to yearn for spiritual perfection. At this time, whenever it came, he was to relinquish even the few comforts of the forest and enter the final stage of life. He was now to become a *sannyasi*—a homeless, possessionless wanderer and beggar.

In the *sannyasi* stage of life a man was the ideal ascetic. He had no worldly attachments, except perhaps to the begging bowl that supplied his one meal a day. To be a *sannyasi* meant ignoring every physical need and every mental distraction. For the purpose of the final stage of life was to cleanse the soul of desire so completely that it could attain *moksha*, release from the cycle of rebirths and reincarnation to which men's souls were bound.

Moksha was the highest of the four goals that, along with the four classes and the four stages of life, were part of the organization of the ideal— the perfect life. The other three goals of life were less mystical. These three goals were *artha*, to acquire material wealth; *kama*, to enjoy all the physical pleasures proper to man; and *dharma*, to perform all of man's proper duties.

A householder was encouraged to be successful. It was proper for him to hurry after wealth on his farm, in the making and selling of goods, or by any other honest means. Pleasure of all kinds was a legitimate and correct pursuit for a virtuous man, and among the pleasures the sexual was unabashedly included. Its skillful achievement was a sacred obligation. A man's dharma consisted of these activities along with the ceremonies and rituals appropriate to each class and stage of life.

The law books recognized that the needs and capacities of men differed according to their class and stage of life; though the goals were the same for everyone, fulfillment of the goals varied. A brahman at the celibate student stage of life might find kama, physical pleasure, in studying the Vedas; for a kshatriya student, kama was more likely to be found when he practiced his skill with a bow and arrow. An eager vaishya merchant sought artha, wealth, at his shop or at the wharves where the trading ships came in; the shudra servant achieved artha when he caught the cast-off clothing his master tossed to him.

A picture of an ideal unchanging society at the time of creation could not, of course, fit a very real society in constant evolution. From the start, the brahmans who worked out the structures of classes, stages and goals began to allow for subclasses and for differing patterns of conduct. Acknowledging the vagaries of human nature, they tried to account for every social contingency —even paradoxically, for conduct that they themselves banned. Thus, the *Laws of Manu* described a category of "mixed class" for children born of forbidden interclass marriages. They stipulated "times of distress," when members of one class could do the work of another class. They furnished regulations for married students with homes of their own, who visited teachers only for lessons.

But even such provisions could not make the brahmans' vision of life fit the facts. India in the age of the sutras was filled with vibrant men and women who laughed when they were tickled, cried out when they were hurt, and sometimes awoke in the morning too grouchy to be polite to a passing holy man. Some of them were elegant, educated men-about-town who knew dancing, dueling, calligraphy and most of the other 64 arts of graciousness meticulously listed in the *Kamasutra*. Some were rough farmers, still scratching subsistence from the land and living in mud huts. Others were busy merchants, professional men—or thieves.

Such people could no more live by formula than people in any other society. As Hindus, they all believed in the concept of dharma and accepted the inequalities inherent in the concept. But to them, the dharma-prescribed system of ideal classes was no more than a religious philosophy translated into everyday language. The system served them as a spiritual framework for their lives: every Hindu could identify himself as brahman, kshatriya, vaishya or shudra; many attempted to pass through the four ideal stages of life and to pursue the four ideal goals. But within this ideal framework Hindus continued to live in very real social patterns that had been worked out long before the brahman manuals of instructions made their appearance. These patterns, which arranged the peoples of India into literally hundreds of segregated groups, are so old and so complex that scholars can only guess at their origins and development.

There are any number of speculative attempts to explain how the real patterns of Indian segregation grew up. A tendency toward segregating groups by occupation apparently existed in pre-historic Indian societies—perhaps even among the people of the pre-Aryan Indus Valley culture. But it was not occupation alone that bound such groups together; they had enough social cohesion to maintain different customs and languages even after they were overwhelmed by Aryan conquerors. The enormous racial pride of the Aryans, in fact, encouraged the separation of peoples, and non-Aryan craftsmen, who banded together to guard the secrets of their craft, apparently came to supervise all the other aspects of the behavior of their groups.

By the end of the Vedic Age, when the brahmans became the arbiters of Indian life, the habit of remaining aloof from neighbors was probably deeply ingrained in old groups and quickly acquired by new ones. Invading tribes that settled in various areas of India retained their own customs, even though they were given a permanent place in Hindu society. The Rajputs, for example, turned so Hindu that they ultimately came to exemplify the "kshatriya," or warrior, in descriptions of the ideal class structure—yet they kept their customs of eating meat, drinking liquor and acquiring wives by abduction.

Whatever the true historical explanation of Indian segregation may be, the principle and the fact of segregation came to dominate Indian society. Hundreds of segregated groups proliferated into hundreds more; in modern times, sociologists distinguish about 3,000 such segregated groups. Obviously, not all the groups come into contact with one another every day. A single village may contain only a dozen different groups; a region, only a hundred or two. But wherever men live in India today, the groups exist, and they set the tone of Indian life as they did 2,000 years ago.

This visible system of segregated groups got the name of "caste" from 16th Century Portuguese travelers, who applied their own word for "clan"

ARTS OF LOVE AND LIFE

Sweetening her breath with a perfumed substance, a lady follows a practice recommended by the *Kamasutra* (literally, "Pleasure Manual"), an Indian classic on love and social conduct. Instructing leisured men and women on sex, etiquette and the choosing of a mate, the book recommends many polite accomplishments as requisites to proper living, among them:

Spreading and arranging beds or couches of flowers . . . upon the ground.

Proper disposition of jewels and decorations, and adornment in dress.

Making lemonades, sherbets . . . and spirituous extracts with proper flavor and color.

Playing on musical glasses filled with water.

Applying perfumed ointments to the body, dressing the hair with unguents and perfumes, and braiding it.

Composing poems . . . [and mastering the] various ways of gambling.

The ability to know the character of a man from his features.

Acknowledgment of society's rules, and of how to pay respects and compliments to others.

or "family" to the society they observed in India. "No one changes from his father's trade, and all those of the same *casta* of shoemakers are the same," reported one such traveler, Garcia de Orte, groping to fit the Indian scheme into a familiar context. The European word has been the foreigners' term for India's social arrangements ever since. (Indians themselves are more precise in their terminology. They use the term *varna*, "color," for their ideal system and *jati*, literally "birth," for the actual system of caste groups.)

Every one of the thousands of Indian castes has traditionally regulated cooking and dining, marriage and occupation. Of these three areas, curiously, the matter of cooking and dining is paramount. In fact, a primary impulse behind the caste system was probably the fear of spiritual pollution through food.

The idea of spiritual pollution is one of mankind's oldest beliefs, and nearly every primitive society seems to have associated such defilement with the magic properties of food. Civilizations far removed from that of India held that the *mana*, or "soul-stuff" of human beings was the same as the soul-stuff of food, especially vegetable food. Unbroken cereal food—grasses growing in a field, seeds waiting to be gathered—retained their soul-stuff when they were handled; anyone could touch and eat them safely. But once grain was softened in cooking or seeds were pressed for their oil, their soul-stuff mixed with the soul-stuff of the person who prepared the food.

Such beliefs usually fade as a society grows sophisticated, but they seldom disappear entirely. In India, the beliefs never abated.

There, food has always been thought to possess an ability to transmit spiritual infection. A taboo on sharing food with an outsider—that is, with anyone not in a man's own caste—was a protective measure against such spiritual pollution.

As a result, even today, each caste has a set of complex rules determining who may cook the food its members eat and who may serve them water. An orthodox brahman, for instance, will eat grain cooked in water only if the cook is another high-caste brahman. He will eat vegetables prepared in ghee—clarified butter—by cooks from castes immediately below his, but he will not eat with these cooks. In addition, a caste determines what its members are permitted to eat. Some castes eat fish but not meat. Others eat neither meat nor fish but will eat eggs. Generally, the higher a caste, the more restricted its menu. The highest castes usually eat only vegetables.

Since a man was hardly likely to marry a girl whose table he could not share, Indian food taboos may also have led to a flat ban on intercaste marriage. In time, however, caste marriage prohibitions acquired so many permutations and combinations that the laws about who could marry whom became as complicated as food laws. Even within castes, there evolved marriage lines that could not be crossed. In the Saraswat brahman caste, for example, a man traditionally may marry his cousin; among Madhyandina brahmans, however, such a marriage would be incestuous. Until very recently, among the Nambudhri caste of southern India, only the eldest son could marry at all; his brothers, by custom, made liaisons with women of the Nair caste (by whom they had children but from whom they could not accept a meal). So convoluted did marriage restrictions become that there are now some castes whose members cannot marry outside 15 families.

The third element of caste, hereditary occupation, entangles the Indian economy in a similar web of restrictions. There are castes of laundrymen, moneylenders, potters, gardeners, oil-pressers, thieves, whores—the list is well-nigh endless. Nearly every job in the economy, from exorcising demons to sweeping the streets, has one or more castes for which that work is reserved.

Though hereditary caste occupation is fundamentally fixed, it does respond to changing conditions. Frequently, the response takes the form of a subcaste. When prehistoric Aryans began to switch from living as nomads in tents to living as settlers in houses, the woodworker caste that whittled tent pegs threw off a subcaste that became that of the carpenters. At other times, a caste adjusts to a new era. Members of the Kayastha caste, a caste of scribes, may have helped disseminate the edicts of Ashoka throughout the Mauryan Empire around 200 B.C., and taken notes in the courts of the imperial Gupta rulers around 350 A.D. They were secretaries to the Mughal emperors around 1550, and became clerks under the British around 1800. Today, a young member of the Kayastha caste may journey to America to study electronic communications.

To a great extent, these unchanging or very slowly changing occupations represent one of the strengths of the caste system, for the very fact of specialized caste occupations led to a smooth-running interdependence among all castes. Carpenters built houses for farmers, farmers sold produce to laundrymen, laundrymen washed the clothes of Rajputs. This interdependence created an economically viable society among groups of people whose lives never touched except at the working level. And in spite of that total social separation, it also induced a great toleration for neighbors whose habits and customs were different, even offensive.

The caste system made one other great contribution to Indian life: it gave its members a sense of security. For example, the caste assumed all financial responsibility for everyone in it, from the aged to the infant; even an incurably lazy young man was often housed, fed, clothed and protected by the members of his caste. Each caste had its own legal machinery to punish wrongdoers within the caste and to defend caste honor outside. If a member of a merchant caste were to receive an inexcusable insult from, say, his landlord, his fellow merchants would pack up their merchandise and close their shops until the injury had been atoned for and the landlord punished—through the legal processes of his own caste of landlords.

Interdependence, stability, a body of shared values—these are the strong points of the caste system, but they had to be paid for. The price of stability, for example, may be stagnation. Hereditary occupations have made Hindu craftsmen resist technological advance because, as British anthropologist J. H. Hutton puts it, an innovation in method appears sometimes as if it were "a sin against the craftsman's ancestors." In a larger sense, a system that fixes a man's status and occupation at the moment of his birth may work against the economic betterment of a whole society. The upward flow of talent is blocked, and the progress of society as a whole often must be made in spite of the caste system rather than in cooperation with it.

The caste system also brought with it the political handicaps of a society based upon segregation. Cut off from one another by barriers of caste, Hindus have suffered from the divisive effects of the only social pattern to which all of them could give their allegiance. India's age-old legacy of political disunity, and the ease with which alien invaders have repeatedly conquered the subcontinent, can be explained in part by the failure of the caste system to provide a single focus of national life.

But the darkest aspect of the system stems from the very root of segregation itself: the fear of pollution, of spiritual defilement, particularly on the part of the brahman leaders of Indian society. Fed over thousands of years by the sacred literature and over countless generations by tradition and law, this fear led to enormous inequalities among the members of the various castes.

In the hierarchy of the caste system, every caste was considered either more or less pure than every other caste, and a man's social status and relationships were determined by his caste's degree of purity. Some castes were so bereft of purity that the very sight of them defiled all other castes. Members of the Chandala caste, for example, could not leave their isolated quarters or villages without striking a wooden clapper to warn of their contaminating approach. On the other end of the same spectrum, some brahman castes held themselves so pure that contact with a member of almost any other caste could make them spiritually unclean. Such brahmans sometimes dined in wringing wet clothes that they had washed themselves, because permitting the garments they wore at meals to dry on a clothesline invited pollution from the shadow of a passerby.

Obviously, attitudes as extreme as these were damaging to the members of all castes, the high as well as the low. But it was among the so-called outcastes or exterior castes—"once-born" castes so low in status that they were held to be outside the pale of human society—that the caste system did its greatest harm. For the members of such castes, who were often forbidden even to use the public roads lest their shadows defile their "twice-born" superiors, life was one long humiliation—a humiliation no less degrading for the fact that most outcastes acquiesced in it. Subservient, almost always illiterate, usually poverty-stricken, these "untouchables" exhibited the effects of the caste system at its worst. Only in very recent times, as caste lines have begun to weaken and laws against untouchability have been passed, has this aspect of the balance between caste's strengths and weakness begun to be redressed.

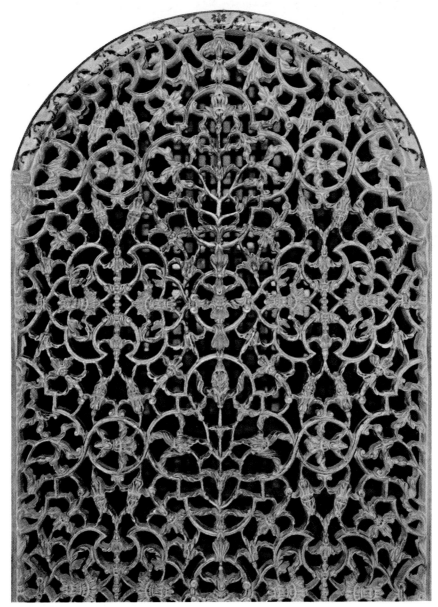

THE INTRICATE DESIGN *of a pierced marble screen shows the fine work done for Shah Jahan.*

A LABOR OF LOVE

Grief-stricken when his favorite wife died during childbirth in 1631, Shah Jahan, one of India's richest and most powerful emperors, determined to build her a mausoleum "as beautiful as she was beautiful." Through 19 years of marriage she had been his constant companion; she was called Mumtaz Mahal, "Chosen of the Palace." To build her a suitable monument, 20,000 expert craftsmen and laborers, summoned from all over India, Asia and even Europe, worked for 22 years. Shah Jahan, a Muslim, based his mausoleum on Islamic concepts, but native materials, motifs and craftsmanship were what finally gave the building its special quality. It is a brilliant fusion of Muslim and Hindu styles, the jewel in India's architectural diadem: the Taj Mahal.

EXQUISITELY PROPORTIONED, *from minarets at each corner to central dome, the Taj Mahal is mirrored in a reflecting pool. Located on the banks of the Jumna*

River near Agra, it was built of white marble brought from Markrana, 250 miles away. The red sandstone buildings are a mosque (left) and an assembly hall.

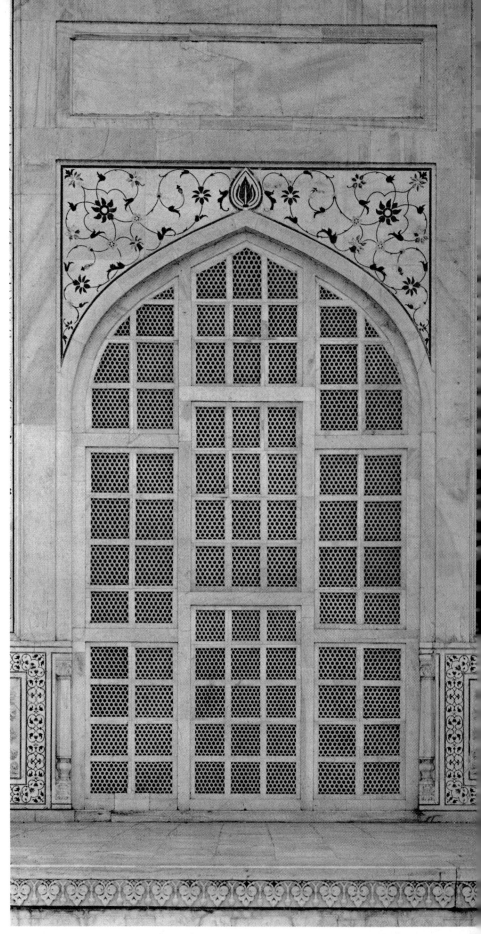

GRACEFUL PATTERNS *of Muslim derivation, including arabesques and chevrons, decorate the octagonal faces of the Taj Mahal. Kiosks encircle the main dome, their tops capped by lotus blossoms, an ancient Hindu motif.*

A RICH MARRIAGE OF STYLES

Nowhere in the Taj does the subtle blending of Islamic and Hindu ideas show more clearly than on its soaring façades. White marble, rather than the red sandstone used by former Muslim rulers for their palaces and forts, was chosen as the material by Shah Jahan, who had been impressed by the beauty of the white marble buildings he had seen in Delhi and Rajasthan. Pointed arches of Muslim inspiration frame windows and doors, in which are set perforated marble grilles of the type often found in Hindu temples. The arabesques and chevrons on the outside are Muslim patterns, but here they take the form of semiprecious stones inlaid in the marble, a technique imported from Italy and mastered by Hindu artisans.

THE MAIN ENTRANCE *is a pointed Muslim archway filled with delicate marble grillwork.*

SOFT LIGHT AND FINELY CRAFTED MONUMENTS

Inside, away from the glitter of sun on white marble, the Taj Mahal conveys a softer mood. As the light filters in through the lacy grillwork of the doors and windows, the focal point of the Taj is revealed. A pierced marble screen six feet tall surrounds the cenotaphs of Mumtaz Mahal and her husband, Shah Jahan. The cenotaph of the empress (at left in the picture below) is at the exact center of the Taj's interior; it is laid out in perfect symmetry with the entrances, directly beneath the central dome. Shah Jahan had planned to build a similar mausoleum for himself, this one of black marble, across the Jumna River, the two to be linked by a silver bridge. But the emperor never realized his plan and he was buried next to his wife.

The cenotaphs themselves are richly decorated with inlays of semiprecious stones—jasper, lapis, bloodstone—done with such precision that breaks between the stones can barely be seen with a magnifying glass. One flower, only an inch square, has 60 different inlays, which feel to the touch like one smooth surface.

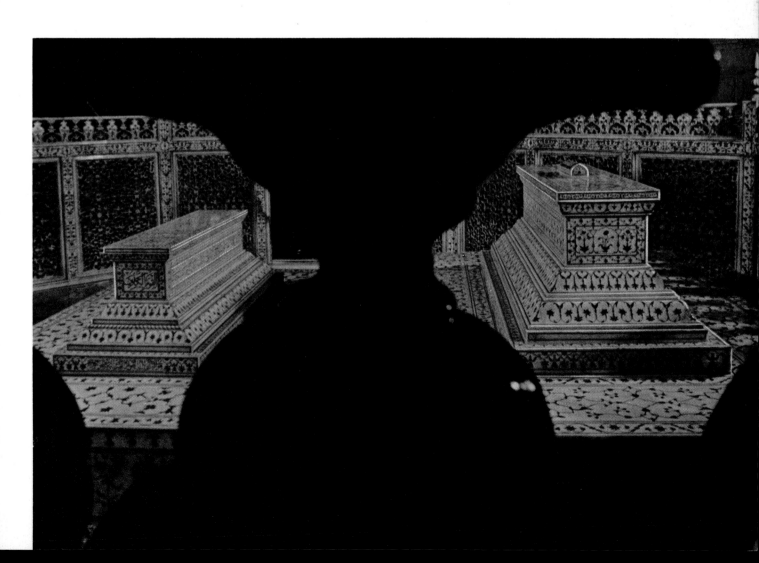

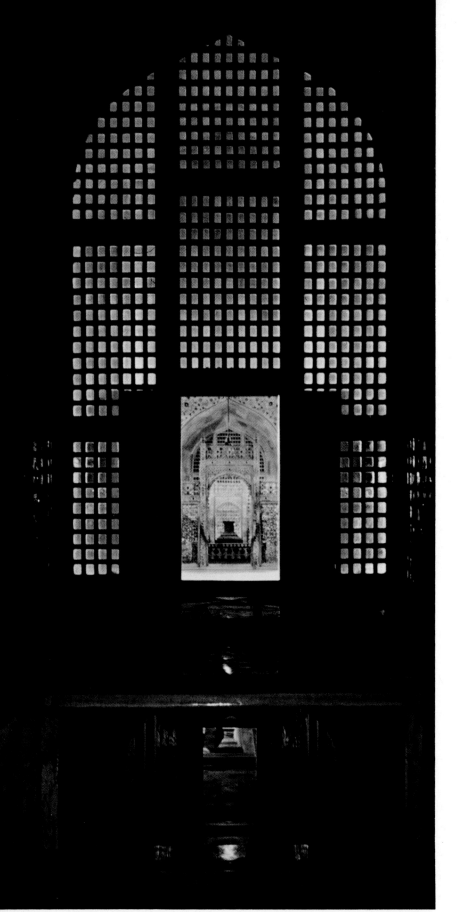

THE BURIAL CRYPT *(right) is beneath the cenotaphs on the main floor. When Muslim rulers were in power, the crypt was opened once a year, and then only Muslims could enter; today it is accessible to everyone.*

THE DARK SERENITY OF THE CRYPT

Below the cool elegance of the Taj Mahal's marbled main floor is a relatively austere burial crypt where the remains of the emperor and his empress lie. Originally the walls and ceiling of the crypt were lined with sheets of gold studded with precious stones. But in the years after the Muslims fell from power, this brilliant ornamentation was stripped from the vault by vandals, along with the canopies of pearls that hung over the coffins and the solid silver doors that sealed the main entrance. The coffins, however, retain their brilliant arabesques, in this case inlays of semiprecious stones so finely and smoothly set that they remained untouched, perhaps because the thieves could not believe the gems were real.

MARBLE FLOWERS
FOR A LOST LOVE

Above all, the Taj Mahal is feminine. Much of its ornamentation, like the beautifully carved marble flowers on the wall of an alcove *(right)*, conveys a sensitive, almost perfumed, loveliness. Both inside and out, the marble reflects the light and mood of the changing day—dazzling at noon, warm and glowing at dusk, soft and ethereal in the moonlight, like the varying moods of a beautiful woman.

It is fortunate that most of this delicate beauty still remains. Within 60 years after the death of Shah Jahan, India dissolved into warring states, marauding bands sacked the monument and Hindu Indians reviled it as a reminder of the hated Muslim overlords. The Taj Mahal was not fully restored until the early 20th Century. Today, however, it is an object of national admiration, and the symbol of India to the entire world.

8
THE MUGHALS' SPLENDOR

If one pattern persisted throughout India's long history, it was the repeated subjugation of Indians by foreign forces—and the turnabout conquest of the conquerors by Hinduism. Beginning as far back as the Third Century B.C., India was invaded by Bactrians, Scythians, Sassanians, Huns and many others; all of them took over, settled down —and in the end accepted Hindu religious attitudes and the Hindu caste system in place of their original ways of life. None could resist the persistence and flexibility of Hinduism's time-tested power. None, that is, until the Muslims appeared.

The followers of Muhammad came to India in three separate waves: Arabian in the Eighth Century, Turkish in the 12th Century and Turkish-Afghan in the 16th Century. All three waves confronted Hinduism with a unique challenge. The invaders brought with them a civilization as secure as India's own—but a civilization that was based on ideas and attitudes diametrically different from those of Hinduism.

Muslims devoted their lives to Islam, or submission to God. The religion of Islam preached a rigid monotheism: there is no God but God and Muhammad is His Prophet. Finally, Islam held that all Muslims were brothers and that all men were equal before God regardless of their class or their color.

Hindus, of course, felt that the search for religious truth was each man's private affair, and whether he found it in God, gods or a godless intellectual concept was no concern of anybody else. Hinduism, then, was flexible in theology, the one area in which Islam was not. On the other hand, Hinduism insisted that social inequality was the law of the universe and that if there was such a thing as blasphemy, it was to be found in the act of tampering with the social order; the belief that brahmans were superior to all other created beings was as sacred to Hindus as it was repugnant to the Muslims.

Eventually the two sets of ideas met in the Mughal Empire, one of the most brilliant empires the world has ever known, but there was little hint of future glory in the early meetings between these disparate cultures. These meetings consisted of adventurous invasions by Arab armies that

THREE MUSLIM EMPERORS, *who ruled India successively during the peak of Mughal power, are shown side by side on canopied thrones. In the center is the greatest of the emperors, Akbar; to his right is his son, Jahangir; to his left, his grandson, Shah Jahan, who commissioned this painting.*

arrived in India's far western regions from Arabia, via Persia, raising the flag of Muhammad for the greater glory of Baghdad. Such armies began to ride out of Arabia in a drive for conquest and conversion soon after the death of the Prophet in 632. Their successors did not come to their panting halt until almost a century later, when they had overrun the Indian territory of Sind, the lower Indus Valley region on the western side of the Thar Desert. There the Rajput warrior chiefs who held sway over northern India stopped the Muslims. Contained by the Rajputs (who promptly forgot them and turned back to internecine wars of honor), the Arabs never crossed the desert into the Indian heartland; they settled in Sind, converting many Hindus and Buddhists to Islam, but generally leaving the tenor of life undisturbed, and ruled firmly for 300 years.

During that time Muslim kingdoms became well established not only in Sind but, more important, throughout all the rest of India's northwestern border regions—Seistan, Baluchistan and much of Afghanistan. These lands had traditionally been buffer states under Hindu political and social influence. Now they became permanently Islamized and functioned as Muslim bases for future attacks on India.

The first such attacks came in 1001, from the Turkish Muslim kingdom of Ghazni, in what is now Afghanistan, ruled by the ambitious, ruthless Mahmud. Seeking wealth for his expanding empire, he chose to acquire it in India and led a series of 17 incredibly merciless raids into India over some 20 years. His strategy was simple and cruel. He raced his brilliantly organized armies through the northwest passes, pillaged Indian cities, ransacked the treasure-laden Hindu temples and sped back to Ghazni "with so much booty, prisoners and wealth, that the fingers of those who counted them would have been tired." So fe-

rocious were these raids that even among modern Hindus the name of Mahmud of Ghazni stands for the quintessence of Muslim brutality.

Mahmud pillaged India only to take its wealth back to his homeland, but his forays so weakened his Hindu opponents that by 1021 he had incorporated the Punjab region of northwestern India into his empire and set up the Punjabi city of Lahore as a provincial capital. A hundred and fifty years later, Lahore was to become the springboard for deeper incursions into Hindu territory.

This second wave of Islam was a true invasion for, unlike the attacks of Mahmud of Ghazni, its goal was not plunder but land. This invasion, also from Afghanistan, was headed by the imperialist-minded Muhammad Ghuri, who aimed to take first the rich Indo-Gangetic plain, and beyond that, as much more Indian territory as his military might could win him. By 1186 Muhammad had defeated the Muslim rulers of Sind, occupied Lahore and prepared to march on Delhi, at the center of the Indo-Gangetic plain.

The threatened area's Rajput rulers, who had forgotten all thoughts of Muslim danger after Mahmud of Ghazni died, gradually came alive to their peril. Although they were less accustomed to repelling invaders than to fighting among themselves—often magnifying minor bickerings into excuses for major campaigns against one another —the Rajputs now organized a confederacy under a great hero, Prithvi Raja, and set forth to stop Muhammad Ghuri at Tarain, north of Delhi. But instead of driving off the invader, the Rajput forces were decimated. They outnumbered the Turks but were hopelessly outclassed. The Turks deployed troops of mounted archers trained to wheel and turn, feint and retreat, then circle around for surprise flank attacks. Against such dangerously mobile forces, the brave but tradition-bound Hindu warriors sent clumsy elephants, and

THE FORTRESS OF JAISALMER *maintains its 800-year-old vigil over a once strategic Rajput city in northwestern India. In the late 13th Century the fort was sacked after an eight-year siege by the Muslim sultan Ala ud-Din. In 1570 it was made part of the Mughal Empire by the Emperor Akbar.*

disorganized massed infantry swinging maces, the same hand-to-hand fighting technique that had served Chandragupta Maurya in the Fourth Century B.C. At Tarain, according to a Muslim observer, "a hundred thousand groveling Hindus swiftly departed to the flames of hell." The Rajputs lost forever their role as defenders of the marches of northern India, and Muhammad Ghuri was free to continue his conquest. His armies, moving southeast, plundered the holy Hindu city of Banaras, ransacked the capital of Bengal and by 1206, when Muhammad died, controlled nearly all of India north of the Deccan. With the permanent occupation of these conquered lands, a new chapter in Indian history began.

Until then Indian lands captured by Muslims had always been considered outposts of empires whose centers lay well outside India. Even Muhammad's territories were merely provinces of his Afghan kingdom of Ghur. But when Muhammad died, his kingdom disintegrated, and the generals he had left to command his Indian territories were isolated from their homeland. Like invaders for thousands of years before them, they discovered that they had arrived in India to stay. With them were many civilian Muslims. Central Asian adventurers and fortune-seekers had followed the victorious armies, streaming down from the far northwest, often with their families. After Qutb-ud-din Aibak, one of these generals, proclaimed Muhammad Ghuri's Indian possessions an independent Muslim kingdom, the influx of civilian Muslims increased until it was almost a true migration. The bulk of this immigration centered on Delhi, where Aibak established his court and where successor dynasties ruled until the 16th Century as the Delhi Sultanate.

The rough Turkish soldiers and carpetbaggers who came storming into India did not bring with them a fully formed culture that was both strong and subtle enough to stand on its own against Hinduism. Despite their allegiance to Islam, the Central Asian Turks were still fairly crude tribes. Whatever cultivation they possessed had been acquired secondhand from the Persians, who had conscripted them as early as the 10th Century; even by the 12th Century such elegance was scarcely more than superficial. Rougher and tougher invaders than these had many times been taken in by the Indian system and smoothed into obedient Hindus—the Rajputs themselves were one example of such converts.

In the usual course of events, Hinduism probably would have transformed the new arrivals as it had done all their predecessors. But suddenly the course of events took an unexpected turn. In the early 13th Century, the Mongols appeared from the steppes of Central Asia. Swift and insensibly cruel, they swept over thousands of miles in a mindless orgy of destruction, terrorizing the whole Eurasian landmass from Japan to Hungary. Under Genghis Khan they ravished Bukhara, Samarkand and the other great Central Asian cities that had flowered with Turkish vigor and Persian culture. They rampaged through the Muslim world as far as Baghdad, where they offhandedly massacred scholars and burned libraries. One of the few Muslim regions to escape the Mongol visitation was northern India, probably because it is protected by mountain barriers. It quickly became a sanctuary for refugees, many of them scholars and artists, for Muslim culture was then one of the most highly developed of any in the world. The gifted refugees flooding into 13th Century India made it the center of a high civilization, a civilization that combined the most advanced Islamic scholarship with strains of older, more traditional intellectual and artistic development rooted in ancient Persia and classical Greece.

Against the strengths of this blended culture,

THE FIRST MUGHAL EMPEROR, *Babur, pauses over a manuscript he is writing. A fierce warrior, Babur (Turkish for "lion") was also a cultivated gentleman who wrote a charming autobiography and encouraged the arts of poetry, gardening and painting.*

Hinduism could make little headway. But neither did it retreat before the power of the ambitious sultans in Delhi who pressed hard against the rest of India. The sultans may have been ennobled by the religious knowledge of the refugees and intellectually stimulated by the richness of Persian arts and mores, but they were still military men addicted to fighting and hungry for conquest. For over a century, they sent steady streams of marauding expeditions and campaigns east and south, conquering the entire Indo-Gangetic plain and establishing their rule in large areas of the Deccan. But the power of the Delhi sultans was uncertain and short-lived. They were not able to control their own Muslim governors in Bengal and the Deccan, who broke away from Delhi and proclaimed themselves independent at every opportunity. Gradually, too, the sultans were forced to realize that the subcontinent they hoped to possess absolutely was resisting them geographically as well as politically, with almost impassable terrain in Rajputana, an almost unreachable but huge area to the south and completely unmanageable elements in-between.

As the sultanate weakened, Hindu kings in Rajputana and southern India also began to reassert themselves. One disgruntled contemporary Muslim wrote that Hindus who had been "so harassed and beaten that they had not even time to scratch their heads now put on fresh apparel, rode on horseback and shot their arrows." The decline gradually steepened and India continued in the type of political organization that, with the few exceptions of the great empires, had always been its condition: a conglomeration of states—some Muslim, some Hindu—continually expanding, consolidating and then disintegrating.

Such a state of affairs was an open invitation to new invaders. By the 16th Century, the weak and inept sultanate was as vulnerable to a takeover from outsiders as the Rajputs had been in the 12th Century. Inevitably the invaders came. Once more they were Muslims, thundering across the Afghan plains and through the mountain passes of India's northwest. Once more, the Muslim invaders were avid adventurers.

This third Muslim wave originally came from a little kingdom in what is now Russian Turkistan. The people were Turkish, although their leader, Babur, traced his lineage back to the famous Mongol chieftains Timur and Genghis Khan (and as a result was called Mongol, which, corrupted, became Mughal).

The brilliant Mughal Empire was about to be formed. Babur and his successors would give India seven generations of extraordinary rulers who, although Muslim, were to fulfill almost better than Ashoka and better than the Gupta emperors, the ancient Hindu dream of the *chakravartin*, or world ruler.

Babur had not originally planned to conquer India, let alone to found one of India's greatest dynasties. His original plan had been to retake all of the great Central Asian empire that his ancestor, Timur, had controlled. But a strong new Persian empire blocked Babur's planned campaigns, and he turned instead to the tempting—and disorganized—northern India. When he attacked the Indian sultan Ibrahim, in 1526, he was outnumbered almost ten to one, and he had no elephants at all against the sultan's 100 elephants. But he had artillery and superior fighting ability. Ibrahim was killed, his armies fled and Babur moved on to occupy Delhi and Agra without resistance. The victorious conqueror then marched on other great centers of northern India, both Muslim and Hindu, met and mastered most Rajput opposition—and, by 1529, had made himself master of the Gangetic plain as far to the east as Patna.

One authority calls Babur "one of the most

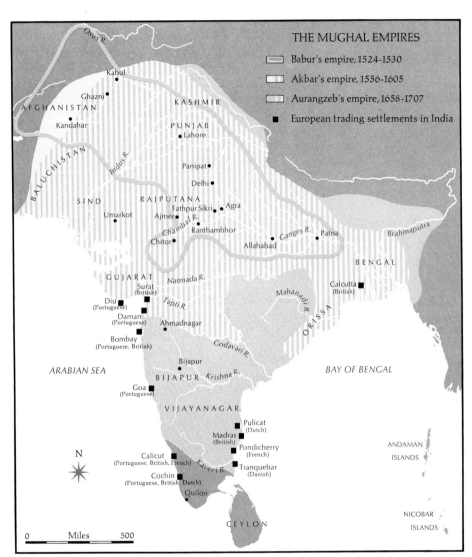

THE MUGHAL EMPIRES

Babur's empire, 1524-1530

Akbar's empire, 1556-1605

Aurangzeb's empire, 1658-1707

■ European trading settlements in India

FOREIGN DOMINATION *was extended slowly over India as the Mughals built a vast empire and European merchants established trading posts along the coasts. The Mughals, a Muslim people who came from what is now Russian Turkistan, carved a large territory in northern India under their first emperor, Babur. Babur's descendants, Akbar and Aurangzeb, spread Mughal suzerainty south, east and west until it covered all the subcontinent except for the southern tip.*

attractive characters in Indian or any other history" and he seems, indeed, to have been a man of delightful personality. One of his first acts in Agra was to lay out a garden—but it was a garden modeled upon Persian examples—for Babur did not especially enjoy his new home. "Hindustan," he wrote in his captivating autobiography, "is a country that has few pleasures to recommend it. The people are not handsome. They have no idea of the charms of friendly so-

ciety, of frankly mixing together, or of familiar intercourse. . . . They have no horses, no good flesh, no grapes or musk melons, no good fruits, no ice or cold water, no good food or bread in their bazaars, no baths or colleges, no candles, no torches, not a candlestick." Yet he charmed his *begs*, or chiefs, into fighting on long after they were disgusted by the heat and dust and dryness and eager to return to the racing mountain streams, the musk melons and the cool valleys of their

Afghan hills. He made a man-to-man appeal to them, and then dramatically smashed his beloved drinking cups as proof of his own resolution to remain in India. (Actually, Babur seems to have employed this device on a number of occasions, but it apparently worked every time.)

The accounts of Babur's death may be apocryphal, but the story is characteristic of him. It says that Babur's son and heir, Humayun, lay dying when a sage told Babur that the boy could be saved if the most precious thing in the world were sacrificed. Babur walked around his son's bed three times, praying, "Oh God, I sacrifice my life, the most precious thing to me, for the sake of the life of my son." Humayun began to get well; immediately Babur himself became ill. The king died in a short time, barely four years after his arrival in India.

Humayun promptly lost control of the territories his father had won. A brother took Babur's Afghan lands and the Punjab. The Afghan governor of a province in northeast India seized Babur's Indian lands. Humayun then began 15 years of exile, roaming Afghanistan and Persia, rounding up support in the fight for his inheritance. In 1555, he returned to regain Lahore and also Delhi, a city much weakened that year by a terrible famine. Humayun died in 1556, leaving an extremely precarious toehold in India to his 13-year-old son, Akbar.

It was Akbar who made the conquests of his grandfather and father into the splendid Mughal Empire. He was so great a man—and emperor—that, as in the case of his contemporary, Queen Elizabeth I of England, history tends almost to remove him from his time and place. Far from being a demigod or mythic hero, Akbar was a shrewd, intelligent and ambitious ruler, blessed with the knack of choosing superb advisors, and he was keenly sensitive to conditions in India.

He was strong-willed—and lucky. When he first inherited his title, his luck was his regent, Bairam Khan, one of Humayun's generals who transferred his fealty and devotion to the young heir. Bairam Khan consolidated the boy's northern Indian territories. But, as one authority says, "Bairam was old and overbearing, Akbar young and masterful." When the boy was 18, they fell out when the young king insisted on exercising his authority, and Akbar then played at being king, rather ineffectually, for a few years. According to one story, his frivolity ended abruptly. One day, irate at a noble who had killed a palace minister, Akbar struck the offender with his own hands and had him thrown over the palace battlements. With that display of personal power, the young emperor immediately became—and thereafter remained—absolute master of his domain.

Akbar's courage and determination became evident soon after he seized absolute power. For one thing, he soon showed dynamic talent as a soldier. Hearing of a revolt in Gujarat, he marched 600 miles from his capital with 3,000 horsemen in nine days, and defeated the insurgents two days later. Such decisive use of his power enabled him eventually to expand his empire until it reached from the Bay of Bengal in the east to Kabul in Afghanistan in the northwest, and from Lahore in the north into the Deccan in the south. But possibly the most remarkable demonstration of his military and political skill was his success in dominating the Rajput Hindu chiefs.

The Rajput domain of Rajputana had always presented special difficulties to Muslim rulers. They could not march south unless the great forts of the Rajputs were secure, for Rajputana lay athwart the routes south from the great Muslim centers of Delhi and Agra. In addition, independent kingdoms so close to the capital could too easily provide sanctuary to royal rebels.

Akbar knew it was necessary to win over the Rajput chieftains—and he also knew they were tenacious opponents. Stubborn and gallant, they could not be overcome by the harsh military measures Akbar used to subjugate Muslim opponents. Compromise was the policy that he chose against these Hindus.

Once a Rajput chief was defeated in battle, he was not deposed but rather made into an ally. Akbar also married Rajput princesses (thus establishing the half-Hindu bloodline of his heirs) and permitted the Hindus full freedom in the practice of their religion. He brought Rajput generals into his court and armies, the most notable being Man Singh, who was appointed viceroy of Kabul and Bengal. By giving the Rajput chiefs a vested interest in Mughal success, Akbar lined them up on his side and was able to use these superior Hindu leaders and their contingents of professional soldiers against the independent Muslim Turkish military commanders who had undermined the sultanate.

The ability to compromise made Akbar master of most of the Indian subcontinent—but it did more. For if the Rajput alliance gave him military protection, compromises in such other areas as taxation, land use, local government and, perhaps most vitally, in religion, stabilized the Mughal Empire and made it the center of a rich and progressive culture.

Akbar, unknowingly emulating the approach of the great Ashoka 18 centuries earlier, realized that he was ruling a multinational, multireligious empire and that the best way to stabilize it was to be equitable. For the peasants, he instituted land reforms that were fair and effective. His officials first made surveys to classify soils and determine the best use of the land. On the basis of this information, they prepared reasonable estimates of farm yields, fixed taxes based upon these yields and carried out honest tax collection.

He halted the destruction of Hindu temples and ended the *jizya,* the discriminatory tax against non-Muslims. Although as a Muslim he had to consider the judgment of the religious leaders, the *ulama,* "those who knew" Islamic law, he weighed their opinions against his own sense of what was best for all of his people, and if there was conflict, he usually set the orthodox ruling aside. Akbar also fostered arts and letters. He encouraged both Hindu and Muslim painters by setting up studios for them at court and by holding weekly showings at which the best artists were rewarded, not only with honor but with money as well. Akbar also supported poetry and was a patron of poets—generally Muslims writing in exquisite Persian, but including an official Hindu *kavi rai,* or poet laureate.

Yet these were not the emperor's favorite interests. Religion, so intrinsic to Indian life, intrigued Akbar perhaps more than any other cultural area. He summoned religious scholars and theologians—brahmans, Jains, Zoroastrians and Jesuits as well as Muslims—for regular Friday afternoon religious discussions. Their disputations apparently made the emperor something of a mystic and freethinker. At any rate, in 1582, when he was 40, he publicly promulgated the *Din Illahi,* a simple and monotheistic religious cult with himself as its center. The cult died with Akbar, but showed clearly how Akbar, like ancient Hindu philosophers, made his own search for religious truth, and in this proved himself thoroughly Indian.

During the 49 years of his reign, Akbar's basic administration became so firmly entrenched that it enabled the Mughal Empire—unlike any earlier one—to develop and expand for 100 years under three less-gifted heirs of the dynasty: the emperors Jahangir, Shah Jahan and Aurangzeb. Jahangir, described as having a "demonic temper [and] a callous disregard for human suffering . . . mingled with a genial temperament," proved the imperial strength by putting down rebellions in Bengal and making that northeast area an important Mughal satellite. He also added to the empire the large Rajput kingdom of Mewar, which had successfully defied Akbar. His son, Shah Jahan, annexed large portions of the Deccan, a major thrust forward, for the sultans of such Deccan kingdoms as Golkunda and Bijapur had previously acknowledged Mughal power by no more than occasional lavish gifts to the court. Final consolidation of the Deccan into the empire was the goal of Shah Jahan's son, Aurangzeb, for whom expansion to the south became a lifelong obsession. When Aurangzeb was emperor, the constant drain of northern resources to pay for his southern campaigns contributed to the ultimate collapse of the Mughals.

Aurangzeb was perhaps the most crucial Mughal emperor after Akbar. For in addition to being a fierce soldier, he was, unlike his dynastic predecessors, a sternly orthodox Muslim. Departing from his great-grandfather's tolerant policies, he alienated the Rajputs, banned the building of Hindu temples, reinstituted the discriminatory taxes against Hindus and instituted anti-Hindu laws dictated by the *ulama*. The combination of his unceasing military expeditions and, more important, the denigration of Hindus, the vast majority of his subjects, made Aurangzeb the last of the great Mughals. He inherited one of the shining empires of world history and after a reign of warfare and conquest left it larger in territory than it had ever been—but on the brink of ruin.

The political and military adventures of Akbar's three descendants ultimately created the largest empire in India's history. It included the entire landmass of the subcontinent excepting only the very tip of southern India. But the conquest and control of territory was not the enduring contribution of these rulers. Far more lasting were their extraordinary cultural accomplishments. For each of the emperors brought a special brilliance to the Mughal court—and the world.

To the weak and dissolute Jahangir goes the distinction of bringing Persian elegance to its flower in India. Jahangir did not exactly intend to do this when he married the Persian noblewoman Nur Jahan and gave her, and her Persian relatives, almost joint control of imperial affairs. So influential did Nur Jahan become that Jahangir used to say that "he had handed her the country in return for a cup of wine and a few morsels of food." Along with the immediate Persian influence came a turn toward lavish living for its own sake. This was a dramatic change from Akbar's way of life, which leaned toward the traditional Hindu emphasis on spiritual and philosophical pursuits, often at the expense of material luxuries. Some of these changes were to exert lasting influences on India, permanently affecting the style of life for both Muslims and upper-class Hindus.

In Jahangir's time Persian manners and mores became the model for all fashionable India, just as French manners and mores in the 17th and 18th Centuries became the model for all fashionable Europe. Persian became the court language and the language of upper-class society. The rough Persian of the troops, intermixed with Indian languages, became Urdu, which remains today the popular language of the Punjab and northern India. Hindus of good family wore Persian clothes and gave their children Persian names. (In our century, the late Indian Prime Minister Nehru was an example of the Persianization of highly placed Hindus: his familiar high-necked jacket, leg-hugging *churidar* trousers and small cap were all Muslim; he spoke the Urdu language in his home; and his given name, Jawaharlal, was Persian.)

However, more noteworthy than any effect on fashion was Persian penetration of the arts. A graceful mingling of Persian-Muslim styles, on the one hand, with Hindu traditions, on the other, led to a distinctive Indo-Islamic style and the creation of some of the world's most beautiful paintings, music and architecture.

The new style quickly proved itself in painting. Humayun had introduced Persian painters into his court at Delhi, having picked them up in his wanderings through Persia, and this talented group attracted Hindu artists, who soon outnumbered Persians many times over. The Hindus adapted the delicate brushwork and other techniques of the Persians to produce miniatures, for example, that are considered by many authorities to be unsurpassed in the art of East or West; they raised portraiture to extremely high levels; and they also used their synthesized technique to paint classic Hindu subjects—the mythology of Vishnu and Shiva, the heroes of the great epics, the *Ramayana* and the *Mahabharata.*

Somewhat the same thing happened to music. Hindu music changed its tune. Borrowing from Persian, Arabic and Central Asian music, it turned from Hindu spiritual themes to the sensuous use of constantly repeated words and musical phrases.

That Mughal music became a truly popular Indian art was a gift from Aurangzeb. When he took over the Mughal court he reinstituted the ascetic Muslim rules that his more liberal predecessors had ignored, and he banned music altogether (even though as a young man he had been exceedingly fond of it). According to a story of the time, the court musicians held a mock funeral for music, passing Aurangzeb's window bearing their instruments on a bier, in a humorous attempt to cajole the ruler into changing his mind. But Aurangzeb responded by recommending that they bury the music very deeply. Taking the hint, the musicians quit Delhi, the capital. Away from the court, they and their successors were influenced by the folk music of the countryside; the resulting mixture of styles, still called Mughal music, became the best-known and most popular mode of musical composition and performance in northern India.

The greatest of the Indo-Islamic arts to bloom at the fertile Mughal court was architecture, and it was Shah Jahan who was the great builder. His treasury apparently overflowed, for he lavished money not only on music and painting, but also on enormously expensive structures, some of which still stand to awe tourists with their magnificence. In Delhi his monuments include the overpowering yet exquisite fortified palace called the Red Fort and the Jama Masjid, a huge mosque. But his finest monument, and one of the greatest achievements of world architecture, was no public building but a tomb—the famous Taj Mahal in Agra.

In 1631 Shah Jahan suffered a great personal sorrow: his wife, Mumtaz Mahal, whom he had loved so ardently that it is said she spent her entire married life horizontal, died at the age of 39 while giving birth to their 14th child. Shah Jahan, wracked with grief—and perhaps, pride—determined that no effort should be spared to make her tomb beautiful. He caused to have built "the miracle of miracles, the final wonder of the world," the Taj Mahal, which is depicted in photographs on pages 142-153.

Such glorious achievements in the arts made the Mughal Empire one of the greatest the world has ever seen. But the ornamental Indo-Islamic culture of the Mughals was only embroidery on the fabric of Indian life. In the villages, where then as now the vast majority of Indians lived, the Indo-Islamic world was remote and the Hindu tradition remained in full force. Governments in Delhi seldom disturbed Indian villagers; both the

EUROPEAN COLONISTS *are seen conversing across a table in a detail from an 18th Century sari that was woven in Bengal. At first, European costumes and customs were considered exotic in India, but eventually they were adopted by the upper classes, particularly by businessmen who dealt with Western industrialists.*

first Turkish rulers and the great Mughals simply substituted one group of tax collectors for another, "changing the men at the top of the social pyramid without upsetting the pyramid itself," as one authority puts it. Even at the height of Muslim rule, village government stayed completely in the hands of Hindu headmen who maintained traditional caste life.

In fact, most Hindus responded to the alien force with what today is called ghetto psychology: they burrowed deeper into their Hinduism. *Bhakti*, the devotional worship, became widespread. The focus of much religious ardor was the great cult of Krishna—the playful infant, the amorous cowherd, the valiant charioteer of Hindu mythology—but the worship of Rama also increased. For the story of Rama, the *Ramayana*, one of the two great religious epics of Hinduism, appeared in the vernacular for the first time during the Mughal reign. Many scholars claim that in the history of India, only Buddha influenced more Indians than the 16th Century poet, Tulasidas, who wrote the new version of the epic. So pervasive was Tulasidas' tale of Rama and so effective was it in reinforcing Hindu beliefs, that Hinduism became stronger among the mass of the people of India than it had ever been before.

At the same time, exaggeration of surface Hindu practices protected the deeper strength of the ancient way of life. For if Hinduism could not overwhelm Islam, neither could Islam completely alter the Hindus. It was not a question of ruler and ruled. It was not the matter of customs and habits. It was not even the obvious difference between Muslim and Hindu attitudes toward God. The impasse between ancient Hinduism and the religion of the newest invaders of India came about because Hinduism held that the way to deal with the pain and sorrow of life was to transcend the social or political situations in which suffering existed, while Islam maintained that man's pain and sorrow were the will of God and must be accepted. This contrast was too fundamental to permit Islam and Hinduism truly to meet. And India was a Hindu land.

In 600 years of political domination, Islam, despite impressive proselytizing, won surprisingly few converts. When the Mughal Empire fell, less than a fifth of the Indian population was Muslim.

Of the Indians who did accept Islam, many had been Buddhists. Those converts who had been Hindus, far fewer in number, were swayed in some cases by special personal considerations. Among the upper castes, ambition was a strong motive. Muslims could more easily rise to the top echelons of government and professions than Hindus. Other caste Hindus, captured in battle and forced to associate with the foreigner and eat his food, might find that they were no longer ritually pure enough to be accepted by their families and castes. Such unfortunates had almost no alternative but to convert.

Some untouchables turned to the brotherhood of Islam, but not in the great numbers that Westerners might expect. In the Hindu world, untouchables knew they owed their lowly status to the faults of previous lives. No matter what Islam promised, most outcastes felt certain that their only way to improve future lives was to be true to their dharmas in this one.

Most conversions came about through Muslim religious ascetics, *sufis*. These mystics were in harmony with Hinduism as well as with orthodox Islam. Unlike the legal-minded Muslim *ulama*, they were constantly searching for their own knowledge of reality. They adopted many of the practices of traditional Hindu asceticism, including meditation and the various disciplines of body and breath control (as well as the less-dramatic habit of using prayer beads). *Sufis* lived alone or among disciples, somewhat in the manner of the holy men—the ascetics and the wandering beggars —of Hinduism, and these Muslim holy men gathered cult converts through the purity of their lives and the meaningfulness of their messages.

Converts from Hinduism kept their past with them. They retained traditional ceremonies; today, Muslim and Hindu marriage ceremonies are almost identical. (At the same time, some Muslims came to accept the idea of a society divided into hierarchical groups resembling castes. Muslim "castes" —Sayyid, Shaikh, Pathan—were not, however, rigid. "Last year I was a Julaha," goes one saying. "This year I am a Shaikh and next year, if the harvest be good, I shall be a Sayyid.") So indoctrinated were the "new Muslims" with their former Hinduism that Muslim farmers regularly called upon Hindu gods for a rich harvest and Muslim women sacrificed milk and ghee (clarified butter) to the Hindu goddess of smallpox.

In these ways Hinduism infiltrated Islam. Although the essential religious difference between the two could never be bridged, Hinduism still controlled the culture of India. Once again the power of coexistence won over a seemingly conquering force. In fact, mature Hinduism had successfully met its first serious challenge.

With the diminishing of the Mughal Empire still another of the endless cycles of Indian time would turn and new invaders once again appear. They would arrive, not through the northwest mountain passes, but on ships; their purpose would be trade and not conquest of land. Like their predecessors they would come in waves— first the Portuguese, then the British—and they would have their centuries of triumph.

But once again Hinduism, which enfolds or patiently, passively resists any culture that comes in contact with it, would have the final triumph.

EXPLOITS OF AKBAR

Akbar the Great, he called himself. Conqueror of territories from the Himalayas to the Deccan, he unified Muslims and Hindus into the Mughal Empire of the 16th and 17th Centuries, governed wisely and actively supported the arts. Yet he never learned to read. When he commissioned a history of his reign he ordered one he could enjoy: a book, called the "Akbarnama," that amplifies text with pictures. Its vivid illustrations trace Akbar's life from his birth to Queen Maryam Makani (in yellow shawl below) until his maturity as a cultivated ruler.

From birth, young Akbar's life was a melodrama of perils and deliverances. While his father struggled to regain the throne and territory that had been seized by rival chieftains, Akbar at an early age experienced the vicissitudes of war. Once he was left behind with servants when his parents were compelled to flee from pursuing troops on a single horse across the desert wilderness; later, as a hostage, he was pushed to an exposed position high in the enemy's fort so that his father's relief army had to cease firing. Ultimately, however, his father's forces prevailed and Akbar was free to pursue his princely education in riding, fencing and shooting. His elderly guardian was Bairam Khan, who is shown in this picture (top center) instructing him in the intricacies of the musket, while courtiers marvel at his skill. Although he encouraged Akbar's passion for reciting Islam's mystical poetry, the royal guardian and his scholars failed completely to teach the youth reading or writing.

Akbar was 13 when his father died suddenly and he inherited the throne. But he did not let his new responsibilities prevent him from continuing to live dangerously, both in battle and around

the table. He became fond of palm wine and even stronger drinks made with opium and spices. Several drafts of one of these concoctions often led him to take risks that terrified his courtiers. One day when he was 19 he rode a vicious elephant into combat against another elephant, pursuing the beast across the Jumna River over a fragile floating bridge before ending the chase. On another occasion Akbar was barely saved from death when, in the incident illustrated at the right, he took the idle challenge of a drinking-party conversation seriously. His companions praised the suicidal bravery of the Rajput warriors, whose land Akbar had just conquered. As a form of dueling, two dare-devil Rajputs would run from opposite sides toward a double-headed spear held by a third person, and impale themselves on the weapon simultaneously. In a flush of bravado, Akbar announced to his astonished friends that he would run himself against a sword fixed on a wall. As he began his dash, his relative, Raja Man Singh, kicked down the sword—cutting Akbar's hand but saving his life. In the picture at right, a servant watches aghast from the small drinking room (top) as Akbar (center, in white turban) is restrained from strangling Man Singh in anger.

ometimes Akbar liked to hunt at night with a few torchbearers, seeking out antelope and other game animals with trained cheetahs. But more often he hunted in broad daylight—with so many comrades and retainers that the party resembled an army on the move. Such a hunt, or "kamargha," could serve the function of military maneuvers, preparing men and war animals alike for a battle to come. On a campaign to quell a rebellion in Malwa in 1564, Akbar indulged in a side expedition to hunt and train elephants. The picture at right shows two aspects of that expedition: at the bottom, an animal that has been captured is lashed between two trained elephants and introduced to the disciplines of army life; at the top, an obstreperous elephant, who would not be subdued easily, is fought by a trained war elephant. Supervising the activity is Akbar (riding a piebald horse), who explains the niceties of the combat to his followers. The biggest "kamargha" that Akbar ever staged was in Lahore in 1567, when some 50,000 beaters worked for nearly one month to drive the game into a

circle 10 miles around for the convenience of the hunters.

While the youthful monarch was still attempting to establish his royal authority, the most direct threat to his sovereignty came from palace retainers, who sought to keep their hold over him. The most ambitious of these was the arrogant Adham Khan, who, as the son of Akbar's nurse, enjoyed the courtesy title of the king's "foster brother." Adham Khan's schemes were jeopardized when Akbar appointed a trustworthy, loyal official as his prime minister. Making their most direct countermove, Adham Khan and a company of conspirators burst in upon the prime minister one day and killed him. As the hapless official lay dying (at lower left in this picture) Adham Khan ran up the stairs to the harem terrace, where he was intercepted. Akbar, roused from a nap in the harem (top left), came forth and knocked Adham Khan unconscious, then ordered him to be bound and thrown into the courtyard below. Unfortunately the work was poorly done, and the rebellious courtier had to be hurled down a second time (center) before he was killed.

The first half of Akbar's reign was devoted to winning military control over the conglomeration of independent and semi-independent principalities that made up India in the 16th Century. After decades of campaigning—characterized by systematic warfare against one powerful stronghold after another—Akbar eventually ruled a realm that extended from the Himalayas to the Deccan and from the Persian border to Southeast Asia.

Akbar's tactical skills and determination were demonstrated at the Rajput stronghold of Ranthambhor, a seemingly impregnable fortress atop a mountain. First, Akbar's engineers built a formidable base for the attack (visible at lower right in this illustration). While snipers and sappers moved forward against the walls, cannon fire from this base set parts of the great fortress ablaze, throwing the Rajputs and their war elephants into turmoil (upper left). Meanwhile, Akbar sought another position from which to shell the Rajput redoubt. As the picture on this page shows, he yoked 200 teams of oxen together, put drummers astride the cannon to sound out the beat, and with a sweaty team

effort had his bulky and heavy cast-iron cannon pulled up the narrow ravines of the surrounding slopes to commanding hilltops. After a siege of 37 days, Ranthambhor was in flames and on the point of capitulating when it was visited by a strange embassy. Since Rajput tradition guaranteed safety for neighboring princes who wanted to parley during a war, Akbar sent forth his ally, Raja Man of Amber, who was duly admitted to the fortress. With the raja came a humble mace bearer—Akbar in disguise. But while the official meeting was taking place, Akbar's identity was discovered. Rather than lose his composure —and perhaps his head too— Akbar simply suggested that it would be better for everyone if the fortress surrendered, and promised to reward Ranthambhor's rulers with high offices. His cool offer was accepted, and another province was thereby added to the vast territories of the Mughal Empire.

But Akbar had not always been such a merciful victor; on other occasions he demonstrated his ruthlessness, most brutally perhaps during the conquest of the mighty Rajput fortress of Chitor. Enraged by the ferocity of the defense, after overrunning the fortress Akbar ordered a general massacre in which over 30,000 Hindus were killed.

While he was still carrying out his conquest of northern India, Akbar was presented with good news of a different sort: the messengers crowding into this picture from the upper left have come to Akbar's camp to tell him that his wife, Maryam Zamani, has just been delivered of a son. That joyous report, greeted by a banging of drums and a whirling of local maidens, marked the successful culmination of Akbar's endeavors to come to terms dynastically with the power systems of the great Hindu states. Early in his campaigns, Akbar had realized that, in order to govern effectively the lands that he had conquered, he had to win the cooperation of the Rajput ruling caste, as well as the allegiance of Hindus of all classes. He therefore adopted a series of enlightened measures, most noticeably the abolishment of the hated "jizya," the traditional tax on all non-Muslims. Moreover, he won the favor of the high-ranking Rajputs by investing them with titles and commands—and by courting and marrying their daughters. But for years Akbar was painfully frustrated in his desire to have an heir to his throne. Then, dur-

ing a pilgrimage to a Muslim shrine, he met a holy man from Sikri, who assured him that his prayers would be answered. In 1569, when Akbar learned that Maryam was with child, he sent her to the holy man's house at Sikri, where in August a boy was born. He was named Salim, after the holy man; but as a son Prince Salim proved to be a mixed blessing to his father.

At Sikri, Salim's birth (top left in this illustration) was marked by the clashing of cymbals, the blowing of many trumpets and the distribution of alms to the poor (bottom). However, Salim became cruel, rebellious and more devoted to alcohol and opium than to his father's principles. As Akbar grew in age and wisdom, he became more and more interested in religion—both that of Islam and of other peoples. In 1578 he invited Jesuits from Portuguese Goa to acquaint him with the gospels. Finally he devised a synthetic religion called "Divine Monotheism," derived from Islam, Hinduism and Zoroastrianism. But like his son Salim, "Divine Monotheism" turned out to be one of Akbar's children that never quite prospered.

To commemorate Salim's birth and also to provide a fitting capital for his growing empire, Akbar decided to abandon his headquarters at Agra and to establish a new capital at Sikri (100 miles south of modern New Delhi). Construction of the new city, whose name later was changed to Fathpur ("Town of Victory"), was begun in 1569 and went on for 15 years. Akbar took personal charge of various phases of the design and construction; at the top of the picture at right he is seen conferring with the architect, while various artisans engrave slabs, prepare building blocks, and make and carry mortar for the walls. Gradually Fathpur Sikri arose, until the gleaming city was a grand and yet delicate composition of schools, public buildings, bath houses, palaces, temples—all interspersed with the terraces and gardens that were a basic part of the capital's Persian-influenced architecture. Akbar's own throne hall was a two-story pavilion of red sandstone. Through the windows he could see a central courtyard with a pool and four bridges extending to an island that held a stage for court music. Happy as he may have been in his

monumental capital, Akbar was destined to be disappointed in it, too. Early in the 1580s, however, it was discovered that Fathpur Sikri's water supply was inadequate; in 1585 the capital was abandoned and is presently nothing but a magnificent ruin.

Perhaps the most significant monument to Akbar was the vast empire that he governed so wisely for 49 years. But the most enduring tribute to his cultural leadership was the variety of art that flourished under his able patronage. Painters, architects, musicians, poets, theologians and historians crowded the court, vying for the emperor's attention. His assertive personality is reflected particularly in the new look of the paintings produced by his hundreds of court painters: in them one can trace an evolution from the subtle and decorative Persian style to the considerably more turbulent and dynamic Mughal style. This lively style illustrated the "Akbarnama," which was completed during the early 17th Century. The scene at right shows the work, being presented to Akbar, who is surrounded by his illustrious company: artists, intellectuals, warriors, poets and sportsmen of many hues and many lands.

CROSSROAD CIVILIZATIONS BETWEEN EAST AND WEST

The chart at right is designed to show the duration of historic Indian civilization, and to relate it to others in the "Crossroad" group of cultures that are considered in one major group of volumes in this series. This chart is excerpted from a comprehensive world chronology that appears in the introductory booklet of the series. Comparison of the chart with the world chronology will enable the reader to relate India's historic culture to important cultural periods in other parts of the Far East and to Western exploration and colonization.

On the following pages is a chronological listing of important events that took place in the period covered by this book.

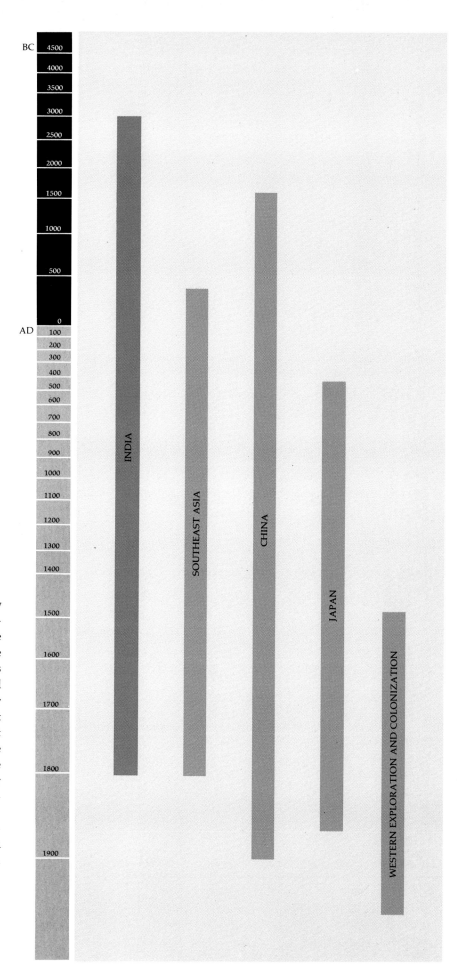

CHRONOLOGY: *A listing of significant events in historic India*

B.C.	Politics and Society		Thought and Culture
2500	Indus Valley civilization flourishes, with capitals at the cities of Mohenjo Daro and Harappa		Carved seals and bronze and terra-cotta figurines are produced by the Indus Valley peoples
	Disintegration of the Indus Valley civilization		
1500	Northwestern India is invaded by the Aryans, a nomadic people from Central Asia		
			The Rig Veda, containing India's earliest sacred Hindu hymns, is composed
1000		VEDIC AGE	
	The Aryans spread their conquests as far east as Bihar and Bengal		The later Vedas, Brahmanas and Upanishads are composed
	The kingdom of Magadha is established in northeastern India		
			The Buddha is born in northern India
	Bimbisara, King of Magadha, conquers adjacent territories		Mahavira, the founder of Jainism, is born in northern India
500	Darius of Persia claims northwestern India as part of his empire		
	Alexander the Great reaches India in the course of his conquests		
300	Chandragupta Maurya founds the first great Indian empire		Buddhist temples and ornamental pillars are erected
			India's earliest treatise on government and economics, the *Arthashastra*, ascribed to Chandragupta's minister Kautilya, is written
		MAURYAN EMPIRE	Megasthenes, an ambassador from Greece, resides at the Mauryan court and writes a detailed account of India
	The Mauryan Empire reaches its peak under the enlightened rule of Ashoka		Ashoka is converted to Buddhism, and his humanitarian edicts are inscribed throughout the Mauryan Empire
			A Buddhist council held at the Mauryan capital codifies Buddhist beliefs
200	Greeks from Bactria establish kingdoms in the Punjab and the Indus Valley		Early versions of India's great epics, the *Mahabharata* and the *Ramayana*, are known to exist
	Parthians from Persia invade northern India		
	Scythians from Bactria invade northern India		The *Bhagavad Gita*, the most sacred Hindu poem, is composed
0			
A.D.	Kushans from Central Asia invade northern India		India's most famous early legal code, the *Laws of Manu*, is compiled
			Schools of sculpture at Gandhara and Mathura produce the first images of the Buddha
300	The Pahlava kingdom is established in southern India, and lasts for over 500 years		
	Chandragupta I rules in Magadha, founds the Gupta dynasty		
			Murals are painted in caves at Ajanta and Ellora in the Deccan
			The decimal system is invented by an Indian mathematician
400	Golden Age of Hindu culture flourishes under Chandragupta II		Sanskrit poetry and drama achieve their peak
		GUPTA EMPIRE	Fa-hsien, a Buddhist traveler from China, visits and reports on the Gupta court
			Kalidasa writes distinguished Sanskrit poetry and drama
	White Huns from Central Asia war against the Guptas		Jain oral traditions are codified
			The great Buddhist monastery at Nalanda is founded
	The second White Hun invasion destroys the already weakened Gupta Empire		Hindu astronomers know that the earth is round and rotates on its axis
500			

Politics and Society

Thought and Culture

600	

King Harsha of Kanauj revives northern Indian culture

The Chalukyas establish a dynasty in the Deccan and rule, with occasional interruptions, for 500 years

The Chinese traveler Hsuan-tsang visits and reports on Harsha's court

The Rajput kingdoms, small independent states, rise in the north and thrive for more than a thousand years

700

Conquest of Sind by Arabs brings first Muslim rule to India

Buddhism spreads to Nepal and Tibet

Dandin writes ornate Sanskrit prose

The Pala dynasty begins its lengthy rule of Bihar and Bengal

Elaborate temples are built at Bhuvaneshvar in northern India

The philosopher Shankara interprets the Upanishads

900

The Chola Empire at Tanjore asserts control in southern India

1000

The Muslim Turk, Mahmud of Ghazni, raids India, conquers the Punjab and annexes the Arab Sind kingdom

The philosopher Ramanuja writes about devotion to the gods

Other Turkish Muslims, the Ghurids, capture Mahmud's possessions in India and rout the Hindu Rajputs.

1200

The Ghurids, under Iltutmish, establish the Delhi Sultanate

The Delhi Sultanate is consolidated by Balban

The important temple at Konarak in northern India is erected

The Delhi Sultanate carries its rule into southern India

1300

Marco Polo visits India

The Vijayanagar kingdom is established in southern India

Lalla, poetess of Kashmir, writes songs to Shiva

Timur (Tamerlane) invades northern India and sacks Delhi

1400

Kabir composes poems urging religious and social reform

Nanak, the founder of Sikkhism, is born

Vasco da Gama lands at Calicut, seeking spices

1500

The Portuguese establish a trading colony at Goa

Babur, founder of the Mughal dynasty, conquers India from the Punjab to the borders of Bengal

St. Francis Xavier proselytizes in India

Mirabai, Rajput poetess, writes songs to Krishna

Akbar, the greatest Mughal emperor, brings unity and peace to northern India and conquers part of the Deccan

Persian ideas combine with local Indian tradition to create the Mughal school of miniature painting

1600

British East India Company is incorporated

Tulasidas of Banaras translates the *Ramayana* into Hindi

Dutch East India Company is chartered

Reign of the Mughal Emperor Shah Jahan

The Taj Mahal, crown of Mughal architecture, is built

Under Aurangzeb, the Mughal Empire achieves its greatest territorial extent

The French establish an East Indian trading company

1700

Decline of the Mughal Empire begins

The Mughal Empire collapses

MUGHAL EMPIRE

A HINDU PANTHEON

Among the remarkable achievements of Hinduism was its blending of the countless cults, gods and totems of India's many ages and diverse peoples into one vast mythology—a mythology dominated by the two Hindu gods, Shiva and Vishnu.

The roster of these deities reaches, quite literally, into the millions. It includes all the gods of early sacred and epic literature and their later permutations; deified mortals; and the animals, birds, trees, mountains, rivers and plants revered as divine personalities by India's primitive tribes.

The characteristics of many of these gods often merged into one. Shiva, for example, incorporates aspects of the fertility-god of the prehistoric Indus Valley people, as well as the fierce god Rudra of the early Aryan invaders and the unnamed dance-gods of the Dravidians of the Tamil region. When such adopted gods were too disparate to be combined, they were simply made members of the families of important gods or incarnations (avatars) of them. Animals venerated by the earliest Indian societies—the bull, the elephant, the serpent—were joined to the Hindu pantheon as the companions of the major deities. A few of the best-known and most widely worshiped of these deities, avatars and companions are noted below.

SHIVA

BRAHMA THE CREATOR, *once thought the greatest of the gods because he set the universe in motion, faded in importance with the rise of Shiva and Vishnu. He appears in white robes and rides a goose. From his four heads sprang the Vedas, which he carries along with a scepter and various other symbols.*

SHIVA THE DESTROYER, *one of Hinduism's two mightiest gods, represents power whatever his aspect—the fierce ascetic; the demon-slayer entwined in snakes and wearing a headdress of skulls; the Lord of Creation, dancing in a circle of fire; the male symbol of fertility. He, more than other gods, is a composite of older gods, cults and myths reaching back to India's prehistory.*

PARVATI *(or Mahadevi), Shiva's wife, was the daughter of the Himalaya Mountains and the sister of the river Ganges. With love, she lured Shiva from his asceticism; she represents the unity of god and goddess, man and woman.*

UMA *is the golden goddess, a creature of light and beauty, who, as a form of Parvati, reflects milder manifestations of her husband, Shiva. She sometimes mediates conflicts between Brahma and the other gods.*

DURGA, *who is Parvati as a ferocious 10-armed goddess, sprang full grown from the flaming mouths of Brahma, Shiva and Vishnu. Astride a tiger, she uses the weapons of the gods to battle demons.*

KALI *is Parvati turned into Hinduism's most terrible goddess, with an insatiable lust for blood sacrifice. She usually appears blood-smeared, bedecked in snakes and wearing a necklace of her sons' skulls.*

THE BULL NANDI, *sacred to the Indus people as a fertility symbol, was absorbed into Hinduism as Shiva's constant companion—his mount, his chamberlain, his musician. Shiva wears Nandi's emblem, the crescent moon, on his brow.*

KARTTIKEYA *(or Skanda) replaced the Vedic god Indra as the principal Hindu god of battle. The son of Shiva and, in some myths, begotten without a mother, he is interested only in fighting and war. Six-headed and 12-armed, Karttikeya leads his celestial legions from the back of a colorful peacock.*

GANESHA, *the roly-poly elephant-headed son of Shiva, is probably the most popular god in the pantheon. Wise, thoughtful and well versed in the scriptures, he is invoked by worshipers before every undertaking to assure success.*

PARVATI

VISHNU

VISHNU THE PRESERVER—*and to many Hindus, the Universal God*—usually holds four symbols: a discus, a conch shell, a mace and a lotus. Whenever mankind needs help, this benevolent god appears on earth as an avatar, or reincarnation. It is generally believed that nine avatars have already appeared; a tenth is yet to come. Some feats of the avatars reflect Indian history.

THE HORNED-FISH MATSYA *represents Vishnu's intercession at a time of universal flood. The fish warned Manu (the Hindu equivalent of both Adam and Noah), then saved him in a ship hooked onto his horn.*

THE TORTOISE KURMA, *the second avatar of Vishnu, appeared on earth after the flood to retrieve treasures, including the ambrosia of the gods. The tortoise churned the ocean, bringing up the ambrosia.*

THE BOAR VARAHA, *originally the sacred pig of a primitive cult, became an avatar of Vishnu after a second flood. Digging underwater with his tusks, the boar raised the earth and restored it to dry land.*

THE MAN-LION NARASIMHA *was another avatar of Vishnu. Brahma had given a demon invulnerability day and night against god, man or beast. The avatar—god, man and beast—killed the demon at dusk.*

THE DWARF VAMANA, *another avatar, became a giant to foil a demon who sought control of the universe. Granted permission to keep all he could cover in three steps, Vamana encompassed the earth, sky and middle air.*

PARASURAMA *was Vishnu as the son of a brahman robbed by a kshatryia king. Parasurama killed the king, whose sons, in turn, killed the brahman. Parasurama then killed all male kshatryias for 21 generations.*

RAMA, *the hero of India's great religious literary epic, the "Ramayana," was Vishnu as an avatar who overcame the world's most terrible demon, Ravana. Rama represents the ideal Hindu: a gentle husband, a kindly king and, most significantly, a leader valiant under oppression.*

SITA, *Rama's wife, an incarnation of Lakshmi, represents the ideal Hindu wife. She was abducted by the demon Ravana and taken to his abode, but remained devoted to her husband.*

HANUMAN, *the monkey king, lent his agility, speed and strength to Rama to help free Sita from Ravana. In return, he asked to live as long as men remember Rama; thus, Hanuman is immortal.*

KRISHNA, *Vishnu's most important avatar, was a hero-god beloved in many aspects: a prankish child, an amorous adolescent, a mature hero who spoke the great lessons of the "Bhagavad Gita." These aspects of Krishna had different origins: Aryan, Dravidian, perhaps Christian.*

BUDDHA, *as an incarnation of Vishnu, exemplifies Hinduism's ability to absorb disparate religious elements. The avatar Buddha appeared, Hindus say, primarily to teach the world to have compassion for animals.*

KALKIN, *the avatar of Vishnu yet to come, is pictured on a white horse, punishing evil-doers and rewarding the righteous. Some Hindus look to his arrival as some Christians do to Christ's Second Coming.*

LAKSHMI, *Vishnu's wife, often shown both sitting on a lotus and holding a lotus, represents good fortune. Her attendants are two gentle elephants. An important goddess in her own right, she is also worshiped as the avatar Sita.*

GARUDA, *Vishnu's mount, is a mythical white-faced bird with the head and wings of an eagle and the body and limbs of a man. Carrying the god on his flashing golden back, he was sometimes mistaken for the fire-god, Agni.*

RAMA

KRISHNA

BIBLIOGRAPHY

The following volumes were selected during the preparation of this book for their interest and authority, and for their usefulness to readers seeking additional information on specific points. An asterisk (*) marks works available in both hard cover and paperback editions; a dagger (†) indicates availability only in paperback.

GENERAL HISTORY

Abul Fazl, *The Akbar-nama (History of Akbar).* Transl. by H. Beveridge. Asiatic Society, Calcutta, 1907.

Auboyer, Jeannine, *Daily Life in Ancient India from 200 B.C. to 700 A.D.* Transl. by Simon Watson Taylor. Macmillan, 1965.

Basham, A. L., *The Wonder That Was India.** Hawthorn Books, 1963.

Binyon, Laurence, *Akbar.* D. Appleton & Co., 1932.

Davies, C. Collin, *An Historical Atlas of the Indian Peninsula.* 2nd ed. Oxford University Press, 1959.

Hutton, J. H., *Caste in India.* 4th ed. Oxford University Press, 1963.

Ikram, S. M., *Muslim Civilization in India.* Ed. by Ainslie T. Embree. Columbia University Press, 1964.

Karve, Irawati, *Hindu Society, An Interpretation.* Deccan College, Poona, India, 1961.

Lamb, Beatrice Pitney, *India: A World in Transition.** Frederick A. Praeger, 1965.

Leifer, Walter, *Himalaya, Mountains of Destiny.* Gallery Press, London, 1962.

Majumdar, R. C., gen. ed., *The History and Culture of the Indian People.* Vols. 1-7. Paragon Book Reprint Corp., 1951, 1954, 1960.

Nehru, Jawaharlal:
Discovery of India.† Ed. by Robert I. Crane. Doubleday Anchor Books, 1960.
Glimpses of World History. The John Day Company, 1942.

Piggott, Stuart, *Prehistoric India.* Barnes & Noble, 1962.

Smith, Vincent A.:
Akbar, The Great Mogul. S. Chand & Co., New Delhi, 1966.
Asoka, The Buddhist Emperor of India. S. Chand & Co., New Delhi, 1964.

Spear, Percival:
A History of India.† Vol. 2. Penguin Books, 1965.
India: A Modern History. University of Michigan Press, 1961.

Thapar, Romila, *A History of India.†* Vol. 1. Penguin Books, 1966.

Wheeler, Mortimer:
Civilizations of the Indus Valley and Beyond. McGraw-Hill, 1966.
Early India and Pakistan to Ashoka. Frederick A. Praeger, 1959.

ART AND ARCHITECTURE

Barrett, Douglass, and Basil Gray, *Painting of India.* Skira, World Publishing Co., 1963.

Brown, Percy:
Indian Architecture (Buddhist and Hindu). Tudor Publishing Co., 1963.
Indian Architecture (Islamic). D. B. Taraporevala Sons & Co., Bombay, 1964.

Coomaraswamy, Ananda K.:
The Arts and Crafts of India and Ceylon.* Farrar, Straus, 1964.
History of Indian and Indonesian Art.† Dover Publications, 1965.

Davar, Firoze C., *Iran and India Through the Ages.* Asia Publishing House, 1962.

Fabri; Charles, *An Introduction to Indian Architecture.* Asia Publishing House, 1963.

Frederic, Louis, *The Art of India, Temples and Sculpture.* Harry N. Abrams, 1959.

Goetz, Hermann, *The Art of India.* Crown Publishers, 1964.

Gupte, Ramesh Shankar, and B. D. Mahajan, *Ajanta, Ellora and Aurangabad Caves.* D. B. Taraporevala Sons & Co., Bombay, 1962.

Kramrisch, Stella, *The Art of India.* 3rd ed. Phaidon Publishers, 1965.

Marshall, John, ed., *Mohenjo-Daro and the Indus Civilization.* 3 vols. Arthur Probsthain, London, 1931.

Mookerjee, Ajit, *The Arts of India, From Prehistoric To Modern Times.* Charles E. Tuttle, 1966.

Randhawa, M. S., *Kangra Paintings of the Bhagavata Purana.* National Museum of India, New Delhi, 1960.

Rowland, Benjamin:
The Ajanta Caves. UNESCO, Italy, 1963.
The Art and Architecture of India. Penguin Books, 1967.

Smith, Vincent A., *A History of Fine Art in India and Ceylon.* 3rd ed. Tudor Publishing Co., 1963.

Speiser, Werner, *Oriental Architecture in Color.* Viking Press, 1965.

Welch, Stuart C., *The Art of Mughal India.* The Asia Society, 1963.

Welch, Stuart C., and Milo C. Beach, *Gods, Thrones, and Peacocks.* The Asia Society, 1965.

Wheeler, Mortimer, ed., *Splendours of the East.* Donald Moore Books, London, 1965.

Yazdani, G., *Ajanta.* 4 vols. Oxford University Press, 1930-1955.

Zimmer, Heinrich, *The Art of Indian Asia.* 2 vols. Bollingen Series No. 39. Pantheon Books, 1955, 1964.

RELIGION AND LITERATURE

Archer, E.W.G., *The Loves of Krishna.* Macmillan, N. D.

Berry, Thomas. *Buddhism.* Hawthorn Books, 1967.

The Bhagavad Gita: The Song Celestial. Transl. by Edwin Arnold. Heritage Press, 1965.

DeBary, William T., and others, eds., *Sources of Indian Tradition.** Columbia University Press, 1958.

Embree, Ainslie T., ed., *The Hindu Tradition.* Modern Library, 1966.

Gerber, William, ed., *The Mind of India.* Macmillan, 1967.

India, Government of, *The Way of the Buddha.* Publications Division, Ministry of Information & Broadcasting, N. D.

Ions, Veronica, *Indian Mythology.* Paul Hamlyn, London, 1967.

Kalidasa:
The Cloud Messenger.* Transl. by Franklin & Eleanor Edgerton. University of Michigan, 1964.
Shakuntala and Other Writings.† E. P. Dutton, 1959.

The Kama Sutra of Vatsyayana.† Transl. by Richard F. Burton. Dutton Paperback, 1964.

Keith, A. B.:
A History of Sanskrit Literature. Oxford University Press, 1928.
Religion and Philosophy of the Veda and Upanishads, 2 vols. Harvard University Press, 1925.

Lal, P., ed., *Great Sanskrit Plays in Modern Translation.** New Directions Books, 1964.

Legge, James, ed., *A Record of Buddhist Kingdoms.* Dover Publications, 1965.

Macnicol, Nicol, ed., *Hindu Scriptures.* Dutton, Everyman's Library, 1963.

The Panchatantra.* Transl. by Arthur W. Ryder. University of Chicago Press, 1956.

Radhakrishnan, *The Hindu View of Life.* Unwin Books, London, 1960.

The Ramayana and the Mahabharata. Transl. by R. C. Dutt. Dutton, Everyman's Library, 1966.

Ross, Nancy W., *Three Ways of Asian Wisdom.* Simon & Schuster, 1966.

Sen, K. M., *Hinduism.* Penguin Books, 1962.

Smith, Huston, *The Religions of Man.** Harper & Row, 1958.

Thomas, Edward J., *The Life of Buddha As Legend and History.* Barnes & Noble, 1952.

Thomas, P., *Epics, Myths & Legends of India.* Tudor Publishing Co., 1963.

Zaehner, Robert C., *Hinduism.** Oxford University Press, 1966.

Zimmer, Heinrich, *Myths and Symbols in Indian Art and Civilization.* Ed. by Joseph Campbell. Harper Torchbooks, 1965.

ACKNOWLEDGMENTS

For help given in the preparation of this book, the editors are particularly indebted to Ainslie T. Embree, Associate Professor of History, Department of History, Columbia University. The editors are also grateful to Jane Gaston Mahler, Associate Professor of Art History, Columbia University; Walter Fairservis, Research Associate, Department of Anthropology, American Museum of Natural History, New York; Alice and Nasli Heeramaneck, New York; Welthy H. Fisher, New York, Founder and Director of Literacy Village at Lucknow, India; Stuart Cary Welch, Fogg Art Museum, Harvard University, Cambridge; Pratapaditya Pal, Keeper of Indian Collections, Department of Asiatic Art, Museum of Fine Arts, Boston; Josephine G. Burke, Reporter, Life Magazine; Government of India Tourist Office, New York and Madras, India; Leo Lionni, Genoa, Italy; A. Ghosh, Director General, Archaeological Survey of India, Government of India, New Delhi; C. Sivaramamurti, National Museum, New Delhi; Ajit Mookerjee, Director, Crafts Museum, New Delhi; Department of Tourism, Government of India, New Delhi; Khaliq Adman Nizami, Professor, Aligarh Muslim University, Aligarh, Allahabad, India; Raymond Pannikkar, Professor of Philosophy, Banaras Hindu University, Varanasi, India, and Visiting Professor of World Religions, Harvard School of Divinity, Harvard University, Cambridge; Romila Thaper, Reader in History, University of Delhi, Delhi, India; Irawati Karve, Department of Sociology and Anthropology, Deccan College Post-Graduate and Research Institute, University of Poona, Poona, India; Pandit Ram Mohan Shastri, Varanasi, India; Indian Section, Victoria and Albert Museum, London; the Department of Oriental Manuscripts, the British Museum, London; Chester Beatty Library, Dublin; Museum Für Völkerkunde, Munich; Friedrich Rauch, Munich; International Institute for Comparative Music Studies and Documentation, Berlin.

ART INFORMATION AND PICTURE CREDITS

The sources for the illustrations in this book are set forth below. Descriptive notes on the works of art are included. Credits for pictures positioned from left to right are separated by semicolons, from top to bottom by dashes. Photographers' names which follow a descriptive note appear in parentheses. Abbreviations include "c." for century and "ca." for circa.

COVER—"Lady Enticing a Peacock," miniature painting, from Punjab Hills, probably Kangra Style, ca. 1780, collection of Mrs. John F. Kennedy (Henry Groskinsky). 8-9—Map by Étienne Delessert.

CHAPTER 1: 10—Vrikshaka (Lady of the Tree), from Gyaraspur, Madhya Pradesh, sandstone, 11th-12th c., Central Archeological Museum, Gwalior (J. R. Eyerman for TIME). 12—Dancing Girl, from Mohenjo Daro, bronze, 2500-1700 B.C., National Museum, New Delhi (Larry Burrows). 15—Map by Rafael D. Palacios. 16-17—James Burke. 19—Brian Brake from Rapho Guillumette. 20-21—Stephanie Dinkins. 22-23—Pete Turner; Tomas Sennett. 24—Brian Brake from Rapho Guillumette. 25—E. S. Ross. 26-27—E. S. Ross. 28—Brian Brake from Rapho Guillumette. 29—Lynn Millar from Rapho Guillumette.

CHAPTER 2: 30—A Priest-King or Deity, from Mohenjo Daro, steatite, 2500-1700 B.C., National Museum of Pakistan, Karachi (Larry Burrows). 32—Map by Rafael D. Palacios. 34-35—City map by Donald Crews, after Stuart Piggott, courtesy of Thames and Hudson; diagram of Great Bath, from Sir John Marshall, *Mohenjo Daro and the Indus Civilization*, London, 1931, by permission of Arthur Probsthain, copyright Government of India—cross-section of drain by Donald Crews. 41—Pectoral, from Mohenjo Daro, steatite, 2500-1700 B.C., National Museum of Pakistan, Karachi (Larry Burrows). 42-43—Bird, from Mohenjo Daro, terra cotta, 2500-1700 B.C. (Larry Burrows); *Vishnu and Lakshmi Riding Garuda*, miniature painting, 18th c., Staatliche Museen zu Berlin (Ost), Islamische Abteilung (The Hamlyn Group); Tree of Life, bronze, from southern India, 16th or 17th c., Nelson Gallery of Art-Atkins Museum, Kansas City, Nelson Fund (Henry Groskinsky)—Portrait of a Turkey Cock, by Ustad Mansur, miniature painting in tempera and gold on paper, 1612, the Victoria and Albert Museum, London (Derek Bayes). 44—Monkey, detail from *Descent of the Ganges* frieze at Mamallapuram, 7th c. (Lance Dane)—Portrait of a Monkey, from Mewar, Rajasthan, miniature painting, ca. 1700, collection of Stuart C. Welch (Fogg Art Museum, Harvard University). 45—Monkeys at Play, page from *Anwar i-Suhayli* ("Lights of Canopus"), ca. 1570, School of Oriental and African Studies, University of London (Derek Bayes). 46-47—Detail of page from *Bhagavata Purana*, showing Krishna and his brother Balarama with shepherds, from Mewar, Rajasthan, ca. 1700, Prince of Wales Museum of Western India, Bombay (Werner Forman); "Paradise of Krishna," from Rajasthan, painted cotton temple hanging, 17th c., Museum of Fine Arts, Boston, Maria Antoinette Evans Fund, 29.1080 (Herbert Orth); Bull Capital, from Rampurva, sandstone, 322-185 B.C., courtesy of the National Museum of India and Rashtrapati Bhavan (Baldev-Pix)—Ornamental plate, from Hyderabad, cloisonné enamel on gold, 18th c., Rassiga Gallery, New York (Lee Boltin). 48—Ganesha, from southern India, bronze, Chola period, ca. 11th c., Nelson Gallery of Art-Atkins Museum, Nelson Fund (Henry Groskinsky); baby elephant, detail from *Descent of the Ganges*, frieze at Mamallapuram, 7th c. (Lance Dane). 49—"The Summer Elephant," from Bundi, Rajasthan, miniature painting, ca. 1750, Prince of Wales Museum of Western India, Bombay (Brian Brake from Rapho Guillumette).

CHAPTER 3: 50—Raghubir Singh from Nancy Palmer Agency. 52—Figure in shape of a man, copper sheet, from Bisauli, Uttar Pradesh, ca. 1000 B.C., Bharat Kala Bhavan, Hindu University, Banaras (Archeological Department, Government of India). 56—Jain Nativity, detail from a manuscript page, 1475-1500, National Museum, New Delhi (Federico Borromeo). 59—Head of the Buddha, stone, Gandhara period, 2nd c. B.C., Musée Guimet, Paris (Photo Giraudon, Paris). 61—The Great Stupa at Sanchi, 3rd-1st c. B.C. (Eliot Elisofon). 62-71—Details from reliefs on the gates of the Great Stupa at Sanchi. 62—Bodhi Tree (Tree of Wisdom), from back of north gate (Archeological Survey of India, Government of India)—Wheel of the Doctrine, from front of south gate (Raghubir Singh from Nancy Palmer Agency)—Stupa, from front of north gate (Eliot Elisofon). 63—The Four Encounters (also The Great Departure), from front of north gate (Louis Frédéric from Rapho Guillumette). 64-65—Details from Temptation of Mara, back of north gate (Archeological Survey of India, Government of India). 66—Enlightenment, from front of east gate (Raghubir Singh from Nancy Palmer Agency). 67—First Sermon, from front of south gate (Raghubir Singh from Nancy Palmer Agency). 68—Offering of the Monkey, from front of north gate (Eliot Elisofon). 69—Walking on the Waters, from front of east gate (Eliot Elisofon). 70—Conversion of Nobles, from front of north gate (Eliot Elisofon). 71—Parinirvana, from front of north gate (Eliot Elisofon).

CHAPTER 4: 72—Lion Capital, from Sarnath, polished sandstone, 322-185 B.C., Sarnath Museum (Raghubir Singh from Nancy Palmer Agency). 75—Map by Rafael D. Palacios. 78—The Yakshi Sudarsana, stone relief from Stupa at Barhut, 1st c. B.C. (Louis Frédéric from

The Yakshi Sudarsana, stone relief from Stupa at Barhut, 1st c. B.C. (Louis Frédéric from Rapho Guillumette). 81-89—Details from the wall paintings in the Ajanta caves, 400-700, from Ghulam Yazdani, *Ajanta*, London, Oxford University Press, 1930-1955, 4 volumes, color plates by Messrs. Henry Stone and Son, Banbury, reproduced by permission of Mohammad Abdul Waheed Khan, Director of Archeology and Museums, Andhra Pradesh.

CHAPTER 5: 90—Head of a colossal Buddha, from Mathura, Uttar Pradesh, red sandstone, 5th-6th c., Mathura Museum (Burk Uzzle from Magnum). 93—Map by Rafael D. Palacios. 96—Musicians, carved wood, contemporary (Mario Andi). 99—Detail from Ajanta, Cave 26 (Roloff Beny, courtesy Thames and Hudson). 100-101—Exterior view of Ajanta, Cave 26 (Eliot Elisofon), with drawing by Rudolph Freund. 102-103—Drawings of Bhuvanesvhar Temples by Rudolph Freund; Lingaraj Temple (Eliot Elisofon). 104—Detail from Mukteswara Temple at Bhuvanesvar (Ian Graham). 105—Detail from Rajarani Temple at Bhuvanesvar (Sunil Janah). 106-107—Aerial view of Sun Temple at Konarak (Eliot Elisofon) with drawing by Rudolph Freund; wheel detail (Johnson and Hoffman, Calcutta). 108-109—Detail from Devi Jagadambi Temple at Khajuraho (Archeological Survey of India, Government of India); Kandariya Mahadeo Temple at Khajuraho (Dr. Lino Pellegrini)—floor plan of Lakshmi Temple at Khajuraho, from Louis Frédéric, *The Art of India*, courtesy Arts et Métiers Graphiques, Paris. 110-111—Arunacalesvara Temple at Tiruvannamalai (Eliot Elisofon).

CHAPTER 6: 112—Siva Nataraja, bronze, Chola period, 12th-13th c., Nelson Gallery of Art-Atkins Museum, Kansas City, Nelson Fund. 115—Indra riding Airavata, from Trichinopoly, 1820, Victoria and Albert Museum, London (The Hamlyn Group). 118—Detail from Meenakshi Temple at Madurai (John Lewis Stage). 120—Wash drawings by James Barkley. 123-133—Painting from *Baghavata Purana*, from Punjab Hills, Kangra Style, 1790-1800. 123—"Brahma Begs Pardon of Krishna," National Museum, New Delhi (Raghubir Singh from Nancy Palmer Agency). 124-125—"Krishna Stealing Butter," detail, collection F. D. Wadia, Poona (Raghubir Singh from Nancy Palmer Agency); "The Salvation of Nalakubera and Manigriva," State Museum, Lucknow (Raghubir Singh from Nancy Palmer Agency). 126-127—"Krishna Slays Bakasura," National Museum, New Delhi (Raghubir Singh from Nancy Palmer Agency). 128-129—"Cows Rushing to Meet the Calves," detail, National Museum, New Delhi (Raghubir Singh from Nancy Palmer Agency); "Krishna Swallows the Forest Fire," National Museum, New Delhi (Raghubir Singh from Nancy Palmer Agency). 130-131—"The End of the Tyrant," detail, Chester Beatty Library, Dublin (Jack McManus); "Krishna Slays Kansa," National Museum, New Delhi (Raghubir Singh from Nancy Palmer Agency). 132-133—"The Water Sports of Krishna," Bharat Kala Bhavan, Varanasi (Raghubir Singh from Nancy Palmer Agency).

CHAPTER 7: 134—Detail from a belt pendant, from Rajasthan, silver, gold and turquoise, date unknown, American Museum of Natural History, New York (Lee Boltin). 137—Surya the Sun God, detail from Sun Temple at Konarak, (Roloff Beny). 140—"Princess," miniature painting, from Jaipur, Rajasthan, ca. 1700, collection of Ram Gopal Vijaivargiya (T. Kasi Nath). 143-153—Views of the Taj Mahal. 143—Dr. Lino Pellegrini. 144-145—Pete Turner. 146-147—Federico Borromeo and "Forma e Colore," Florence. 148-151—Larry Burrows. 152-153—Raghubir Singh from Nancy Palmer Agency.

CHAPTER 8: 154—The Emperors Akbar, Jahangir and Shah Jahan with Khan A'zam, I'timad Al-dawlah and Asaf Khan, miniature painting by Bichitr, ca. 1630, Chester Beatty Library, Dublin (Derek Bayes). 157—Lynn Millar from Rapho Guillumette. 158—Detail from a portrait of Emperor Babur, miniature painting, 17th c., Musée Guimet, Paris (Photo Giraudon, Paris). 160—Map by Rafael D. Palacios. 165—Detail from a Baluchar sari, silk brocade, 18th c., Crafts Museum, New Delhi (Raghubir Singh from Nancy Palmer Agency). 167-171—Pages from *Akbarnama* by Abu-l Fazl, original 1602 and 1605 manuscript editions, miniature paintings by various artists. 167-168—Courtesy of the Trustees of the British Museum, London (Heinz Zinram). 169—The Chester Beatty Library, Dublin, photographed at the British Museum, London (Heinz Zinram). 170-176—The Victoria and Albert Museum, London (Derek Bayes). 177—The Chester Beatty Library, Dublin, photographed at the British Museum, London (Heinz Zinram). 182—Parvati, from southern India, bronze, 17th-18th c., Musée Guimet, Paris (Werner Forman)—Shiva Visvantara, from southern India, bronze, 11th-12th c. Musée Guimet, Paris (Werner Forman). 183—Vishnu, from Mathura, red sandstone, 5th c. (Department of Archeology, Government of India)—Balakrishna, from southern India, bronze, 15th c., National Museum, New Delhi (Mario Andi)—Rama, from Vadakkuppanaiyur, Thanjavur, Madras, bronze, 10th c., courtesy Government Museums, Madras (Department of Archeology, Government of India).

INDEX

This symbol in front of a page number indicates an illustration of the subject mentioned.

A

Achilles, comparison with Krishna myth, 115
Adham Khan, *171
Afghanistan, map 160; invasions of India from, 17, 91, 156, 159; Muslim kingdoms in, 156, 157
Agade, trade with, 32
Agni (Aryan god), 36-37, 117, 128
Agra, map 160; in Mughal Empire, 159, 160, 161, 176; Taj Mahal, 145, 164
Agriculture, 51; under Akbar (Mughal Empire), 162; beginnings in India, 31; Harappan crops, 32; and monsoon, 15; spice plantations, 28
Ahimsa (nonviolence), doctrine of, 80
Ahmadnagar, map 160
Aibak, Qutb-ud-din, Indian sultan, 157
Aihole, map 93
Ajanta, map 8-9; cave murals, *81-89; cave-temple, *99-101; cultural center, map 93
Ajmer, map 160
Akbar, Mughal emperor, *154, 161-162, 163; empire of, map 160; government of, 162; illustrations of life of, *167-177; Divine Monotheism of, 162, 175; political accommodation with Rajputs and Hindus, 161-162, 174; warfare of, 161, *172-173
Akbarnama, illustrations from, *167-177
Ala ud-Din, Indian sultan, 157
Alberuni (Muslim scholar), 11
Alexander the Great, 17, 74-75, 91
Algebra, 97-98
Allahabad, 93; in Mughal Empire, map 160
Amaravati, map 93
Amri, map 32
Anaximander, 51
Andaman Islands, map 160
Animals: in arts, 33, *41-49, *68, *72, *82, 94, 95, 99, 105; in fables, 44, 95; husbandry, 35, 41; myths, *42-45, 48; reincarnation in, 41, 54; restraint from killing of, 41, 46, 56, 78, 80; sacredness of all living things, 41, 56, 80; soul of, 41, 53, 55, 56
Antibrahmanism, 55
Anuradhapura, map 93
Aphrodite, comparison of Lakshmi with, 116
Arabia, trade with, 92
Arabian Sea, map 8-9, map 15, 16, map 75, map 93, map 160; Harappan culture sites on, map 32; lifting of coastline, 34; routes to India across, map 15
Arabic numerals, an Indian invention, 18, 97-98
Arabs, invasion of India by, 16, 155-156
Aranyakas, 36
Archeology, 31-32
Architecture: Buddhist cave-temples, *100-101; Gupta period, 91, 94, *100-102; Harappan culture, 32, *34-35; Hindu temples, *102-103, *106-107, 108, *109-111; Mughal (Indo-Islamic), 18, *143-151, 164, *176, 177; Persian influence on, 74, *176; splendor in, 85; Taj Mahal, 18, *143-151, 164
Arjuna (hero of *Mahabharata*), 119-120, 122
Armies: of Mauryan Empire, 77, 80; of Turkish Muslims vs. Rajputs, 156
Aromatics, 28
Artha (goal of life), 138
Arthashastra, 76, 77, 78
Arts, 18; eroticism in, *108, *132-133; Gupta period, 18, 91, 94-97; Harappan culture, *31, 33, *41; iconographic, emergence of, 92, 95; Mauryan period, 18; Mughal period, 18, 162, 164, 177; Persian influences on, 74, 162, 164, *176, 177; Rajput period, 98. *See also* Architecture; Dance; Literature; Music; Painting; Religious art; Sculpture; Temples
Arunacalesvara Temple, near Madras, *110-111
Aryans (Vedic Age), 34-40, 41, 116; early way of life of, 34-35, 40; evolution of Hinduism by, 40, 114; family life, changes in, 40; invasion of India by, 34; kingdoms of, 38-39, 40; language of, 34, table 39; literature of (Vedic), 35-36, 52, 96; meaning of term, 34; religion of, 36-37, 38-40, 54, *115; religious copper object, *53; social order of, 37, 38-40, 139, 141; territorial expansion in India, 38; warfare of, 34-35, 38
Asceticism, *50, 54-55, 121-122; the Buddha and, 58, 67; in hermit stage of life, 138; Hindu, 121-122, 138, 166; Jain, 55-56; Muslim (*sufis*), 166
Ashoka, Mauryan emperor, 78-80, 94, 159, 162; and Buddhism, 79; conquest of Kalinga, map 75, 76, 78-79; edicts and edict sites, 47, map 75, 76, 78-79, 80; empire of, map 75; memorial, *72
Astronomy, 97
Atharva Veda, 36
Atlantis, comparison with Hindu myth, 115
Atman, concept of, 52-53, 55
Aurangzeb, Mughal emperor, 162, 163, 164; empire of, map 160
Avatars, 126
Ayodhya, map 93; kingdom of, 116

B

Babur, Mughal emperor, *158, 159-161; empire of, map 160

Bactrian Greeks, invasion of India by, 91, 92, 155
Baghdad, 156, 158
Bairam Khan, 161, * 168
Balarama (brother of Krishna), *130-131
Baluchistan: in Mauryan Empire, map 75; in Mughal Empire, map 160; Muslim kingdoms in, 156; pre-Harappan settlers, 31
Banaras (Varanasi), map 8-9, 38, 58, map 93, 157
Barabar, map 75
Barley, 32
Basham, A. L., 77, 78, 95
Bengal: in Mughal Empire, map 160, 163; in Muslim Sultanate, 157, 159
Bengal, Bay of, map 8-9, 14, map 15, 16, map 75, map 93, map 160
Bhagavad Gita, 119-121, 136
Bhakti (Hindu worship), 121, 122, 165
Bharata (writer), 96
Bharhut, map 93
Bhuvaneshvar, map 93; Hindu temples at, *102-105, 106
Bible: compared to Hindu epics, 116, 119; compared to Vedas, 36
Bihar Province, *25
Bijapur, map 160; kingdom of, 163
Bimbisara, Magadhan king, 74
Bindusara, Mauryan emperor, 75
Birds, in mythology and art, *42-43
Boccaccio, Giovanni, 95
Bodh Gaya, 95
Bodhi tree, *62, *63, 64
Bolan Pass, map 15
Bombay, map 160
Bonaparte, Napoleon, 74
Brahma (Hindu god), 114, *123
Brahman, concept of, 52, 53, 55, 59, 114, 121; oneness of Atman (individual soul) with, 52-53, 54, 121-122; Ramanuja's view, 122; reconciliation of concept with belief in deities, 114, 121; Shankara's view, 121-122
Brahmanas (commentaries on the Vedas), 36
Brahmanism, 60, 92; expanded to include cults of Shiva and Vishnu, 94, 121
Brahmans, class, 54, *86, 92, 136, 137, 138; caste restrictions, 141, 142; challenged by the Buddha, *69; challenged by Sixth Century B.C. cults, 54-55, 56; codification of social system and dharma by, 135-139; mythical origin of, 40; reassertion of, at end of Kushan rule, 92; reassertion of, at end of Mauryan rule, 80; reassertion over Buddhism, 113
Brahmaputra (river), map 15, map 75, map 93, map 160
British trading settlements in India, map 160, 166
Broach, map 93
Buddha, the, 40, 57-60, 61, 92, 95, 165; caste system ignored by, 59-60, 61, 68-69; deification of, 92; legends about life of, 57-58, 59-60, *61-71; meaning of name, 58, 61; regarded as incarnation of Vishnu by some Hindus, 115; in sculpture, *59, 62, *90, 92, 95; symbols of, *62; teachings of, 58-59, 60, 67-70; temptations of, 58, *64-65
Buddhism, 11, 51, 55, 58-60; changes in, after the Buddha, 60; conversions to Islam, 156, 166; disappearance from India, 60, 61, 113; under Emperor Ashoka, 79; fundamental teachings of, 58-59, 60, 67, 70; influence of Upanishads on, 52, 58; Mahayana, 92; a missionary faith, 79; monasticism, 59, 60, 68; nonviolence, 41, 60; scriptures, 58, 79; sects, 60; spread of, 60, 61, 79
Buddhist Doctrine, Wheel of, *62, *67
Buddhist sculpture, 18, *59, *61-71, *79,

*90, 92, 94-95, *99-101; stupas, *61, *62, 70, *71, 94-95, *101
Buddhist temples, *61, 99, 102; Ajanta caves, *81-89, *99-101
Building materials: Harappan, 32; Mughal period, 147, 176; pre-Harappan, 31
Bukhara, 158
Bulls: in Indian art, *41, *47; veneration of, 41, 46
Burhi Gandak River, *25

C

Calcutta, 14, map 160
Calico, 98
Calicut, map 160
Cambay, Gulf of, map 32
Cape Comorin, map 8-9, 16
Capital cities: Gupta Empire, 94; Harappan culture, map 32, 33; Mauryan Empire, 75, 76; Mughal Empire, 164, *176, 177
Capitals, of pillars of Ashoka, *47, *72, 94
Cashmere, 98
Caste system, 13, 135, 139-142; absorption of invading peoples into, 17, 139, 155; the Buddha's disregard of, 59-60, 61, 68-69; concept of spiritual pollution, 140, 142; and dharma, 136, 138, 139; food restrictions, 140-141; heredity in, 141, 142; Indian terminology, 140; marriage restrictions, 140, 141; Muslim "castes," 166; number of groups, 139; occupational restrictions, 12, 136, 139, 140, 141, 142; origin of, 139; origin of term, 139-140; sacred thread of initiations, *37; strengths of, 17, 141-142; subcastes, 141; untouchables, 142, 166; weaknesses of, 142. *See also* Class system
Cattle: in Indian art, *41, *46-47, *123-129; Hindu protection of, 41, 46; raising of, 15, 35, 41; wealth of Aryans based on, 35, 41
Cave-temples, map 93, 99; at Ajanta, *81-89, *99-101
Central Asia: invasions of India from, 16, 31, 34, 91; Muslim cities of, 158
Ceylon, map 8-9, map 93, map 160; spread of Buddhism to, 79
Chambal River, 14, map 15, map 160
Chakravartin (world ruler), 159
Chandala caste, 142
Chandragupta Maurya, Mauryan emperor, 73, 75-78, 94, 157; ascent to power, 73, 74, 75, 92-93; empire of, 75; reign of, 76-78; turn to Jainism, 78
Chandragupta I, Gupta emperor, 93; empire of, map 93
Chandragupta II, Gupta emperor, 93-94, 97, 98
Chanhu Daro, map 32
Chariot Wheels, in Temple of the Sun at Konarak, *106-107
Chariots, in warfare, 35, 77
Chaucer, Geoffrey, 55, 95
Chenab River, map 32
Chera kingdom, 92
China: in Sixth Century B.C., 51; spread of Buddhism to, 11, 61
Chintz, 98
Chitor, map 160; Akbar's conquest of, 173
Chola kingdom, 92
Christianity, 113, 121; comparisons with Indian thought, 13, 54, 55, 59, 79, 122
Churidar trousers, 163
Cities: growth of, 51; Indus Valley (Harappan) culture, map 32, 33, *34-35
Civilizations, early: pre-Harappan

of social inequalities in, 40; karma, 13, 40, 114, 122; literature, 114, 116-121; meditation, 113, 122; nonviolence, 41, 60; purification baths, *25; Ramanuja's role in, 122; reincarnation, 13, 40, 114, 122; sacrifice, 113; sects, 114; *shakta* cults, 116; significance of Ganges River in, 25; Shankara's role in, 121-122; true Reality, and illusion, 120, 121; worship of Vedic, 36; Mauryan, 76

Jesus, regarded as incarnation of Vishnu by some Hindus, 115
Jewelry, *81-85, *134
Jhelum River, map 32
Jina (or Mahavira, religious leader), 55, *56, 57
Jizya (tax on non-Muslims), 162, 163, 174
Jnatrika clan, 55
Judaism, comparisons with Indian thought, 13, 52
Julaha (Muslim "caste"), 166
Jumna River, map 32, map 93; Taj Mahal on, *144-145
Justice, system of, tied to caste, 142

K

Kabul, map 8-9; in Mauryan Empire, map 75; in Mughal Empire, map 160
Kailash, Mount, 116, 136
Kali (Hindu goddess), 114, 116, 136
Kalibangan, map 32
Kalidasa (poet and dramatist), 97
Kalinga, Ashoka's conquest of, map 75, 76, 78-79
Kalsi, map 75
Kama (goal of life), 138
Kamargha (hunt), *170
Kamasutra (book), 139, 140
Kanauj, map 93
Kanchi, map 93
Kandahar, map 8-9; in Mauryan Empire, map 75; in Mughal Empire, map 160
Kandariya Mahadeo Temple, Khajuraho, *109
Kanishka, Kushan king, 92
Kansa (demon), 126, 130, *131
Kapilavastu, 62, 70, map 93
Karakoram Mountains, map 8-9, map 15, *19-21
Karakoram Pass, map 15
Karli, map 93
Karma, 13, 40, 54, 114, 122; the Buddha and, 60; defined, 54; in Jainism, 55-56
Kashmir, *20-21; in Mauryan Empire, map 75; in Mughal Empire, map 160
Kashmir, Vale of, *19
Kautilya (minister of Chandragupta Maurya), 76
Kaveri River, map 75, map 93, map 160
Kavi rai (poet laureate), 162
Kayastha caste, 166
Khajuraho, map 93; Hindu temples at, *108-109
Khotan, map 93
Khyber Pass, 14, map 15
Kingdoms: Aryan, 38-39, 40, 51; Bijapur, 163; Chera, 92; Chola, 92; of Deccan, 163; Golkunda, 163; Kushan, 92, map 93; Magadhan, 73-74, map 75, 93; Muslim, 156, 157, 159; Pandya, 92; pre-Gupta, 91, 92; of Rajputs, 23, 98, 156, 159, 161-162, 163; of southern India, 92
Konarak, map 8-9; Temple of the Sun at, *106-107
Korea, spread of Buddhism to, 61
Kosala, map 75
Kot Diji, map 32
Krishna (Hindu god), 46, 114, 115, 116, *123; cult strengthened during Mughal rule, 165; discourse with Arjuna, in Bhagavad Gita, 119-121, 122; legends of life of, 115, *124-133
Krishna River, map 15, map 75, map 93, map 160
Kshatriya class, 119, 136, 137, 138, 139
Kulli, map 32
Kumaragupta, Gupta emperor, 98
K'un Lun Mountains, map 8-9, map 15
Kuru tribe, 118
Kushans: invasion by, 91; empire of, 92, map 93

L

La Fontaine, Jean de, 95
Lahore, map 8-9; Ghazni Muslim provincial capital, 156; in Mughal Empire, map 160, 161, 170

Lakshmi (Hindu goddess), 116, 117
Land reforms of Akbar, 162
Land routes to India, map 15
Landscape, *19-29
Languages: Hindi, 39; Indo-European, 34, table 39; Pali, 58; Persian, influence in India, 163; Sanskrit, 18, table 39, 60, 95, 96; Tamil, 92; Urdu, 163; use of vernacular, 60, 165
Lapis lazuli, *149; trade, 32
Latin language, comparisons with Sanskrit, table 39
Laws of Manu, 136-137, 138
Lesser Vehicle (Buddhist sect), 60
Licchavi tribe, 93
Lights of Canopus, The, illustration from, *45
Lingaraja Temple, Bhuvaneshvar, *102-103
Literature: Aryan (Vedic Age), 35-36, 52, 96 (see also Upanishads); drama, 96-97; epics, 116-121, 165; fables, 44, 95; Gupta period, 18, 91, 94, 95-97; Hindu, 114, 116-121; languages, 18, 39, 165; lyric poetry, 95-96, 162; Mughal period, 162, 165
Lothal, 32, map 32

M

Macedonians, in India, 74-75
Madhyandina brahmans, 141
Madras, 27; Arunacalesvara Temple near, *110-111; British trading post, map 160
Madurai, map 93
Magadha, kingdom of, 73-74, map 75, 93
Mahabharata (Hindu epic), 97, 116, 118-121; paintings, 164
Mahanadi River, map 75, map 93, map 160
Mahavira (religious leader), 55, *56, 57
Mahayana Buddhism, 60, 92
Mahmud, king of Ghazni, 156
Malwa, 1564 rebellion in, 170
Mamallapuram, map 93; carvings at, *44, *48
Man of Amber, Raja, 173
Man Singh, Raja, 162, *169
Mana (soul-stuff), 140
Mara (god), 64
Marble, use in Taj Mahal, 18, *143-149, *152-153
Markrana, 145
Marriage, 137; caste-determined, 140, 141; intercaste, 141; interclass, 138; similarity of Hindu and Muslim ceremonies, 166
Maryam Makani, queen, *167
Maryam Zamani, empress, 174, *175
Mathematics, 97-98
Mathura, map 93
Matrilinear societies, 16
Mauryan dynasty, 73, 75
Mauryan Empire, 11, 73, map 75, 76-80, 91, 92; under Ashoka, 78-80; capital of, 75, 76; under Chandragupta Maurya, 76-78; government of, 76-77, 79-80; sculpture, 18, *72, *79, 94; warfare and army of, 77, 80
Meat, restrictions on, 141
Medallion, *134
Meditation, 54, 59, 64, 113, 122, 138, 166
Megasthenes, 76, 77, 78
Merchants (vaishyas), 40, 136, 137, 138
Mewar, 163
Migrations, 14-15. See also Invasions
Miniatures, Indo-Islamic, 164
Missionaries, Buddhist, 79
Mohenjo Daro, map 8-9, map 32, 33-34; city plan, *34; figurine, *30; Great Bath of, *34-35; population figure, 34; seals of, 33
Moksha (goal of life), 138
Monasticism: Buddhist, 59, 60, 68; Jain, 56, 57
Mongolia, spread of Buddhism to, 61
Mongols, 16, 158, 159
Monism, 52-53
Monkeys: in art, *44-45, *68; in fables and myths, 44, *68-69
Monotheism: Akbar's Divine, 162, 175; Islamic, 155; Judaic, 52

Monsoon, 15, 19; Ganges in flood during, *24; wind directions, 28; winds of, over Deccan plateau, *26-27
Moriyas, 73
Mountain passes, 14, map 15, *16-17, 21
Mughal, origin of word, 159
Mughal architecture, 18, *143-151, 164, *176-177
Mughal dynasty, *154, 159, 162-163
Mughal Empire, 159, map 160, 161-166; under Akbar, 161-162; under Aurangzeb, 163, 164; cultural accomplishments of, 18, 162, 163-164; Hindu-Islamic confrontation in, 155, 162, 163, 164-166; warfare, 159, 161, 163, *172-173. See also Delhi Sultanate; Islam; Mughal Empire; Muslim invasions
Mughal music, 18, 164
Mughal painting, 18, 41, *43, *45, *154, 162, 164, *167-177
Mughal plate, *47
Muhammad, prophet, 155
Muhammad Ghuri, king of Ghur, 156-157
Mukteswar Temple, Bhuvaneshvar, *102
Mumtaz Mahal, Mughal empress, 143, 149, 164
Music and musical instruments, *96; Mughal (Indo-Islamic), 18, 164
Muslim invasions of India, 18, 23, 155-159; Arab Muslims, 155-156; Turkish Muslims, 155, 156-158; Turkish-Afghan Muslims (Mughals), 155, 159
Muslim motifs, in Taj Mahal, 143, *146-147
Muslims: and caste system, 166; immigration of, to India, 157; kingdoms of, 156, 157, 159; warfare, 156-157, 159, 161, 163, *172-173. See also Delhi Sultanate; Islam; Mughal Empire; Muslim invasions
Mysore, 75, 78, map 93
Mythology: animals in, *42-45, 48; Buddha, 57-58, 59-60, *62-71; comparisons of Hindu and Western, 115, 116; creation myths, 39-40, 114; Hindu epics, 116-120; Hindu gods, 114-116, *123-133; in Hindu painting, *123-133; in sculpture, *44, *48, *62-71, 95, 99, *104, *106-107

N

Nair caste, 141
Nal, map 32
Nalanda, University of, map 93, 97
Nambudhri caste, 141
Narmada River, map 8-9, map 15, map 32, map 75, map 93, map 160
Nationalism, hampered by caste system, 142
Natyashastra, 96
Negroid inhabitants, early, *12, 16
Nehru, Jawaharlal, 80, 163
Nepal, 62
Nicobar Islands, map 160
Nirvana, 70, *71
Nomadic tribes: from Central Asia, invasion of India by, 31, 34-35; of present, *22-23; transition to agriculture, 31
Nonviolence, doctrine of, 41, 80; in Jainism, 56, 60, 78
Nur Jahan, Mughal empress, 163

O

Occupation, caste-determined, 12, 136, 139, 140, 141, 142
Odyssey, compared to Ramayana, 116
Oedipus, comparison with Krishna myth, 115
Officials, Mauryan Empire, 76, 79
Orissa, map 160
Orte, Garcia de, 140
Outcastes, 142, 166
Oxus River, map 15, map 93, map 160

P

Pahlavas, invasion by, 91
Painting, *42-46, *49; Ajanta cave murals (Buddhist), *81-89; Gupta period, *81-89, 91, map 93, 94; Hindu, *123-133, 164; miniatures, *45, 164; Mughal (Indo-Islamic), 18, *154, 162, 164, *167-177; portraiture, 164
Pali (language), 58
Panchantantra (book of fables), 95
Pandya kingdom, 92
Panipat, map 160
Panis, 38
"Paradise of Krishna," wall-hanging, *46-47
Parthians, invasion by, 91
Parvati (Hindu goddess), 114, 116, 136
Passes, mountain, 14, map 15, *16-17, 21
Pataliputra (Patna), map 8-9; Gupta center of government, map 93, 94; Mauryan capital, map 75, 76, 79; in Mughal Empire, 159, map 160
Pathan (Muslim "caste"), 166
Patna. See Pataliputra
Perseus, comparison with Krishna myth, 115
Persia, 51, 159; cultural influence on and through Islam, 158, 160, 163-164; domination over northwestern India, 73, 74; influence on Indian art, 74, 162, 164, *176, 177; invasions of India by, 16, 74, 91
Persian Gulf trade, 32, 92
Peshawar, map 93
Philosophic concepts: Atman, 52-53; brahman, 52, 53, 114, 121-122; dharma, 13, 54, 114, 136; karma, 13, 40, 54, 55-56, 114; nirvana, 70; reincarnation, 13, 40, 53-54, 64, 114; time concept, 12-13; truth concept, 13
Philosophy, 12-13, 18; of Ninth to 11th Centuries A.D., 121-122; of Sixth Century B.C., 51-52
Pictographs, Harappan, 33
Pillar edicts, of Ashoka, map 75, 76, 78; carved pillar capitals, *47, *72, 94
Poetry: Gupta, 18, 95-96; Mughal, 162
Political development of India, 18, 142
Pollution, spiritual, concept of, 140, 142
Polytheism, 52
Pondicherry, map 160
Population figures: Mohenjo Daro, 34; India, Fourth Century B.C., 14
Ports, Harappan culture, 32
Portuguese trading settlements in India, map 160, 166
Pottery, 135; Harappan culture, 33
Pre-Harappan settlements, 31, map 32
Precious stones, 85; in Taj Mahal, 18, *149, 150
Priests, 36, 37, 38-39, 40. See also Brahmans
Primitive societies, 16, 31; of present, 16, *22-23
Prithvi Raja (Rajput hero), 156
Public works: Harappan (Indus Valley) culture, 32-33; Mauryan period, 78
Pulicat, map 160
Punjab, map 8-9, 14; annexation by Ghazni Muslims, 156; Aryan invasion of, 34; Greek domination over, 73, 74; Kushan kingdom in, 92; language of, 163; in Mauryan Empire, map 75; in Mughal Empire, map 160; Persian domination over, 73, 74
Puramdara (Aryan god), 35
Puri, map 93

Q

Quetta, map 32
Quilon, map 160

R

Radha (incarnation of goddess Lakshmi), 116
Rajarani Temple, Bhuvaneshvar, sculpture from, *105

X

PRODUCTION STAFF FOR TIME INCORPORATED

John L. Hallenbeck (Vice President and Director of Production),
Robert E. Foy and Caroline Ferri
Text photocomposed under the direction of Albert J. Dunn and Arthur J. Dunn